JUST
T·A·L·K

Practical assignments in Oral Communication
for GCSE English

Hilary Caminer & Deborah Catesby

HODDER AND STOUGHTON
LONDON   SYDNEY   AUCKLAND   TORONTO

ACKNOWLEDGMENTS

For permission to quote copyright material the authors and publishers wish to thank the following: Irene Read and the *Guardian* for 'Statistic'; Lindsey Darking for 'A question of marrying and be damned'; William Heinemann Ltd for the extract from *The Grapes of Wrath* by John Steinbeck; Edna O'Brien and Jonathan Cape Ltd for the extract from *Country Girls* by Edna O'Brien; Dougal Robertson and Elek Books for extracts from *Survive the Savage Sea* by Dougal Robertson; Penguin Books Ltd for the extract from *The King Must Die* by Mary Renault; Cherry Gilchrist and B. T. Batsford Ltd for extracts from *Astrology*; George A. Miller and Century Hutchinson Ltd for the phrenological chart from *Psychology: The Science of Mental Life* by George A. Miller; Douglas Adams and Pan Books Ltd for the extract from *Hitchhikers' Guide to the Galaxy* by Douglas Adams; Sue Townsend, Caroline Holden and Methuen Books Ltd for the extract and drawing from *The Secret Diary of Adrian Mole aged 13¾*; *The Times Educational Supplement* for 'Fat of the land' and 'The last Noël' (20.12.85); Jack Straw MP for 'Why this good and bad is ugly'; Victor Zorza for 'Father's ambition for son thwarted by family illness'; ILEA English Centre for the extract from 'Small accidents' by Sabir Mandali; ILEA Learning Materials Service for the extract from *Rights, Responsibilities and the Law* by Judith Edmunds; the Controller of Her Majesty's Stationary Office for the table from *Social Trends 16*; Oxford University Press for the extract from *The Oxford Nursery Rhyme Book* assembled by Iona and Peter Opie, 1955; Liz Lochhead for 'Men Talk'; BBC Publications for the extract from *British Social History: Women's Rights*; Vivienne Tomlinson and the *Radio Times* for 'Too much too young?'; and Martin Plimmer and *Elle* for the article on Jane Tewson.

Thanks are also due to the following for supplying photographs: Sally and Richard Greenhill (pp. 7, 20, 64, 100, 107); Topham Picture Library (pp. 11, 16, 17, 33, (Nos 1 and 4), 34 (Nos 5–7), 57, 75, 76, 77, 87, 99, 108 (bottom left), 109 (bottom left), 111, 113, 117); ET Archive (p. 28); Spectrum Colour Library (pp. 33 (Nos 2 and 3), 118); ITN News (p. 61); BBC Hulton Picture Library (pp. 65, 108 (top and bottom right), 109 (top and bottom right); the *Guardian* (p. 96); Mansell Collection (p. 106); Alan Pascoe Associates (p. 115); and the Anti-Apartheid Movement (p. 116).

British Library Cataloguing in Publication Data

Caminer, Hilary
 Just Talk: practical assignments for and
 communication in GCSE English.
 1. Oral communication—Study and teaching
 (Secondary)—Great Britain
 I. Title   II. Catesby, Deborah
 001.54'2'071241   P95.4.G7

ISBN 0 340 40166 6

First published 1987

Copyright © 1987 Deborah Catesby and Hilary Caminer

Typeset by Tradespools Ltd, Frome, Somerset
Printed in Great Britain
for Hodder and Stoughton Educational
a division of Hodder and Stoughton Ltd,
Mill Road, Dunton Green, Sevenoaks, Kent
by The Eastern Press Ltd,
Reading and London

CONTENTS

INTRODUCTION

This is a book of practical assignments in spoken English. It is designed as a 2-year course book to be used for preparation and assessment for the Oral Communication element of GCSE English.

The book is in two parts. Part I is divided into sections, each of which aims to give practice in different kinds of talking and listening. Section Two, for example, is about working together in groups, talking through problems or dilemmas and coming to joint decisions. Section Five focusses on ways and means of using spoken language in discussion. The subject matter of all the sections is designed to be within the real-life experience or the imaginative scope of young people from 14 upwards.

For many of the assignments in this part of the book, we have suggested that you divide the class into smaller groups. Each assignment gives clear guidance on what is required so that pupils can contribute ideas and experiences within a defined framework. There are also plenty of opportunities for individual work and for work as a whole class.

Part II of the book aims to provide a focus for imaginative and polemical talk and discussion on a series of issues. We have selected these carefully to cater for all kinds of interests and tastes and to allow for varying levels of treatment. The research projects which conclude each of the topics are a good example. You could either use them to stimulate detailed individual investigation in preparation for an oral report or as the basis for informed group discussion. Some of the topics in Part II will probably draw upon ideas raised in other parts of the school curriculum (for example, in Humanities or Science classes, or in books being read for a Literature course).

The book provides an opportunity for enjoyable and interesting talk. The assignments can be used both for practice in oral communication and for formal assessment. We think that they will also provide interesting starting points for written work.

As practising teachers, we are confident that you will find the material in this book easy to use, and that it will provoke imaginative and thoughtful classwork for all GCSE pupils. It will also be useful for the oral elements of Scottish Standard Grade English.

PART I

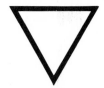

Talking Together

SPEAKING AND WRITING

> MY BROTHER BOBBY'S 10......
> UM.......HE'S GOT RED HAIR

1 Read the extracts printed below. One of them was spoken, and the other written down. What are the main differences between them?

> 'My brother Bobby's 10 . . . Um . . . He's got red hair and a kind of a pudgy sort of face – well, not really pudgy, perhaps it's just fat – he eats too much . . . you know, crisps, sweets, ice cream, that sort of stuff . . . Rubbish – my mum oughtn't to let him eat so much – he can get away with anything, he can – he's really spoilt.'

> My brother's name is Bobby and he's 10 years old. His hair is red and his face is rather fat because he eats too much junk food which isn't healthy. This is because my mother allows him to do whatever he wants; the result is that he's very spoilt indeed.

2 Work with a partner. Each of you should choose one of the subjects given below and then spend 2 or 3 minutes telling your partner about it.

> Your brothers and sisters
> Your pets
> Where you live
> Your first day at school
> Music you like.

Don't think too carefully about what you are going to say; just start talking. If possible, some of you should tape what's said. When you've finished, each of you should write a short paragraph based on what you talked about.

3 What were the differences between what you said and what you wrote? Listen to any recordings that you made and compare them with what you wrote down.

4 What do you think makes somebody interesting to listen to? What makes somebody interesting to talk to?

SECTION

1

TALKING TO AN AUDIENCE

Assignment 1   **Showing how**

| 1·1 |

Instructions   Do you know how to do any of these things?

Play five-a-side football
Make a chicken curry
Dance
Mend a puncture in a bicycle wheel
Eat thirty boiled eggs in half an hour
Clean out a fish tank
Play chess
Do the high jump
Organise a party
Develop and print a film
Groom a horse
Plough a field
Play jacks or hopscotch
Bath a small baby

Here's part of a transcript (a written copy) of someone in a classroom explaining how to swim using the breaststroke:

'You start from the side of the pool. Kick off and hold your arms together and straight ahead of you. Then start moving your arms under the water like this. (DEMONSTRATES) Keep your arms straight. Pull down a bit into the water with your hands slightly sloped so that you're sort of pushing the water behind you. Then bring your arms round and then to the front again so that they're pointing straight ahead of you like this. (DEMONSTRATES) And you go on repeating that. Now the difficult bit. I'm going to show you how to do the legs by demonstrating on Fred, who's lying conveniently on this desk. O.K. Fred? The main idea is that you move your legs a bit like a frog. Can you show them? Can everybody see? He's bending both his knees outwards, shoving the water away with his feet and then

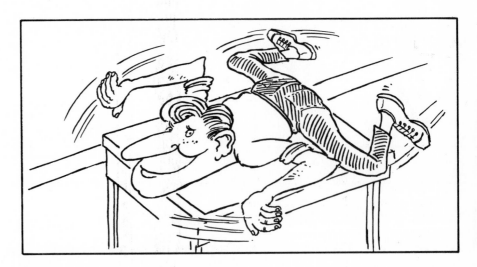

bringing his legs together straight out behind him. Then he starts again. Can you do that a couple of times, please Fred? Everyone get the idea?

Now we'll put the arms and legs together. Start with the arms, and just as you're pulling out and down start your leg kick. O.K. Fred? The idea is that while you're bringing your arms round to finish off the stroke, your legs are still propelling you forward. And while your legs are stopping, your arms are starting. See what I mean? You have to imagine Fred pushing himself through the water.

Show them a couple more times, will you Fred? Now could I have two or three volunteers to try it out on these tables here? Thank you Fred, that was really helpful.'

The most useful part of that talk was probably Fred. Don't be afraid to use visual or human aids or models or props. It's often much easier to show than tell, though you do need words as well.

What aids or props would you use for each of the examples in the list given at the beginning of this assignment? Discuss different ways of explaining some of the examples on the list.

1·2   **Skills exchange**   Choose some fairly simple task or skill that you know about. Plan a demonstration and talk to show the rest of the class how they can learn the skill you're teaching them. Remember to include some way of testing whether they've understood.

Don't write out your talk. It will lack spontaneity and you'll probably lose contact with your audience if you're just reading something out.

It's important, particularly when you're explaining something, to note your listeners' reactions. If they're looking puzzled, you'll need to explain the point again or in a different way.

As a guide to help with the notes for your own talk, here are the ones used for the talk on the breaststroke:

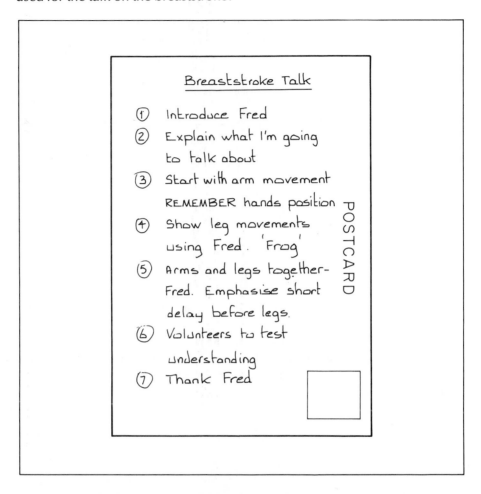

Breaststroke Talk

① Introduce Fred
② Explain what I'm going to talk about
③ Start with arm movement
   REMEMBER hands position
④ Show leg movements using Fred. 'Frog'
⑤ Arms and legs together- Fred. Emphasise short delay before legs.
⑥ Volunteers to test understanding
⑦ Thank Fred

POSTCARD

Of course, this exercise is one that can be spread over a number of weeks, with only one or two people teaching a skill each time.

Assignment 2 **Explaining ideas**

| 2·1 |

The Greyfriars video   Your school has decided to make a video film for prospective pupils and their parents. The aim is to show the range of school activities (for example, drama, music, art, sport, clubs, etc.); the many different kinds of subjects taught (for example, other languages, science, multi-cultural studies, etc.); the facilities and equipment (for example, gym or sports hall, workshops, laboratories, etc.); and some pictures of typical school life.

Here's an example from one school's plan for a similar video:

VIDEO PLAN	
Greyfriars Comprehensive Promotion	
Pictures	**Sound**
Opening shot of front entrance.	This is Greyfriars Comprehensive.
Follow 2 pupils into school and along corridor to assembly. Bustling activity.	Some talk and laughter. Good natured comments from teachers.
Head talking on first day of term.	Brief extracts from welcome to new pupils.
Cut to First Year Humanities Project Work. Lots of maps, pictures, pupils' work on walls. Model of windmill built by pupils.	Questions from class. Discussion on Technology in the Developing World.
Cut to a more formal lesson: Maths. Pupils follow theorem on board. Teacher holding plastic tetrahedron and cone.	Teacher explains and demonstrates part of theorem. Member of class helps in commentary.
Cross cut with English spelling test. Lively but hard working.	Laughter. Final word = 'LABORATORY'.
Cut to Physics lab. Spectacular experiment.	Murmurs. Teacher's voice-over explanation.
Cut to Sports Hall. Trampoline.	Lively, rhythmic music.
etc.	

Why do you think the school chose these particular images to show? Do you think the video would persuade pupils to want to come to the school? What would persuade you to go to a particular school? What would persuade your parents that it was the right place for you?

2·2   **A promotional video**   Stage I – Planning

Working in groups of four or five, make a similar plan for a promotional video for your own school. Before you start, think about the following points:

What aspects of your school would make good television? What would have a strong visual impact?

How many different activities can you show? Can you think of ways of showing most age groups involved in doing something, either in the classroom or elsewhere?

What kind of framework would suit your plans for the video? For example, you could follow one or two pupils through a school day; or you could decide to use a series of fast cuts from scene to scene.

Stage II – Putting the best ideas together

1 When you have finished your plan, prepare a presentation of your group's scheme for the video for the rest of the class. Explain how you are going to organise the video, what pictures you plan to show and the main points you want to communicate. Sum up by pointing out why your ideas are the ones which should be chosen for a final version. Each person in the group should make an equal contribution to your explanation.

2 At the end of your presentation, the rest of the class should comment on what they think of your plan.

3 When everyone has finished presenting their ideas, the class should make a joint plan for a promotional video, taking into account which framework they want to use, and picking out good ideas for pictures and sound effects.

Assignment 3 # Outlining attractions

| 3·1 |

Richmond The London suburb of Richmond Upon Thames has a number of tourist attractions for the foreign visitor. It organises exchanges with the town of Richmond, Virginia in the USA. A group of 15-year-old pupils from that town is planning a visit to Richmond Upon Thames and they are to be entertained by pupils from one of the local schools. The visit is planned to last for 3 days.

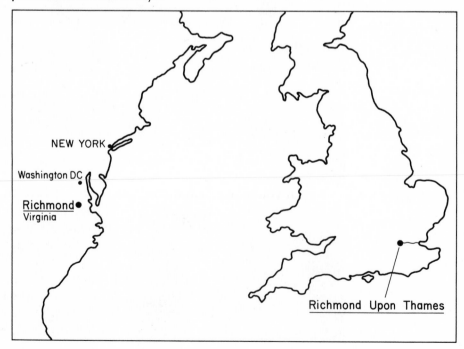

NEW YORK

Washington DC

Richmond
Virginia

Richmond Upon Thames

Four pupils have been chosen by Thameside School to look after the American visitors. Their job is to make them feel welcome, tell them about arrangements, go with them on all visits and deal with problems which come up. They have a member of staff to help them, but the success of the visit is mainly in their hands. Their first task is to welcome the visitors and outline some plans for their visit. Here is a transcript of some of what they said in this introductory talk:

MARY: Good afternoon, everybody. We're from Thameside School and we'd like to welcome you to Richmond-Upon-Thames. We hope you'll have a good time here and go home feeling that the two Richmonds have more in common than just their names. (PAUSE) I'd like to introduce you to your guides for your 3-day visit. That's Matthew over there in the black leather. Don't worry, he's not nearly as frightening as he looks. Then there's Terry. (PAUSE) Where is Terry? Has anyone seen Terry? No? Well, it was going to be Terry but never mind, we'll find someone else . . . Oh, there you are, Terry. And there's Jacqui – yes, all in red – she thinks she's a fire engine – she plays the siren in a band most nights. (PAUSE) Plays the siren? Oh, well, never mind, my mum thought it was funny. And then of course, there's me. I'm Mary. (APPLAUSE) Well, I'm going to hand you over to Terry who's going to tell you about your morning visits to (SOLEMN VOICE) local places of historical interest. Terry . . .

TERRY: You didn't tell me I'd have to get up on to some platform . . . Don't feel safe up here. Right, now what was I supposed to say? (CONSULTS NOTES) Oh yes. Hampton Court. Great historical interest there. You know, Henry VIII . . . You haven't heard of Henry VIII? Six wives, all that stuff? Well, never mind. By the time you get out of Hampton Court at, let's see, 12.30 sharp tomorrow lunch time, you'll have heard of him all right. That is, of course, if you *can* get out. There's a maze, see. In the gardens – sorry, the grounds. And people have been known to get lost for weeks, well, days – hours anyway. Actually it's quite fun. (PAUSE) If you're five. (LAUGHTER) But the arrangements, that's the important thing, isn't it? That's what you want to know. And I must have them here somewhere. (SEARCHES POCKETS) Ah, found them. You have to meet up outside the main gate at 9.30 sharp. We'll all be there to see you round, you lucky people. How do you get there? Easy. Easy. A coach will pick you up right here, outside the school at . . . 9.00 a.m. Got it? Oh, and when you've finished we have lunch on the riverside terrace of a genuine olde worlde English pub. That's if you're out of the maze, of course . . .

| 3·2 | **Introducing your own area** |

What you need: *Local guide books and tourist information*

Your own school is expecting a similar visit from American pupils of your own age. Find out what the local attractions are if you don't know already. Your local library should be able to tell you about historic buildings or parks and you probably know yourselves of unusual walks to take in the daytime and some interesting places to go in the evening.

Work in groups of four or five and prepare an introductory talk for your visitors, based on the suggestions given below:

Suggestions for what to include in your talk

1 An introduction to the four students who will be the main guides. Give more information than Mary did – something about individual interests or school subjects is a help for later conversation.
2 A brief general introduction to your area, giving a few historical details. For example, did anyone famous ever live locally? What are or were the main industries? And so on.
3 An outline of what they will do each day, including some background detail where relevant. You should make clear what kind of visit each will be (outdoors, indoors, historical, artistic, sporting, etc.). You should also say if you're providing a choice.
4 Suggest some entertainment for the evening.

Assignment 4   # Saying what happened

| 4·1 | **'Statistic' – a road accident**   Read the following account, of a real car accident. It's more effective if one person reads the whole thing aloud as if it had happened to him or her. It's a dramatic and realistic account, not for the squeamish. |

Statistic by Irene Read

A feature of modern living is the constant meeting of man and machine. The following commentary on a road accident was published originally in The Guardian *and was issued as a special pamphlet because it reminded motorists very vividly of what such terrible encounters meant for all those involved.*

You have driven this car along this road many times without incident. It is dark, but the road surface is good and visibility is all

right. You are relaxed. The car purrs along superbly because it is a superb car and you are a bit inclined to brag about it to your friends but you are not a fast driver by nature, and really it is a bit wasted on you because you've never had it flat out and you never will, and you're not really the type who has to be first away from the lights or bust. None the less, you're fond of it and proud of it, and proud of the Institute of Advanced Motorists badge on the front. And you haven't even bothered to insure it except for third party because you've been driving for years and you've never so much as scraped an eighth of an inch of paint off any vehicle in your life, and it takes two to make a crash, and you don't ever intend to be the other one. That's the sort of person you are and the sort of car you're in at 10.15 that night. You are travelling at 32 miles per hour, and you know the chap in front is travelling at 32 as well because you've been following him for a long time and he's a good driver. You note that almost subsconsciously because you've done a lot of advanced driving training and they teach you to note everything, and particularly to note the driving behaviour of other vehicles. He's a long way in front, because you never follow anything closely, because that's something else they were very hot about in training. You could have passed him half a dozen times if you'd wanted to, but what's the point? There's no hurry.

He indicates his intention of turning right up a little road that no one ever goes up anyway and you wonder idly what he's going there for. His right flasher is flashing, he pulls to the crown of the road, and he practically stops to let through a southbound vehicle. Your are now approaching what the police driving manual refers to as a

'Hazard'. Ahead is the main road approaching the brow of a hill and bending left. A junction on the right. A car centrally placed about to turn right. The response is casual, relaxed, automatic. Foot off the gas. Cover the brake. Slight reduction in speed. Pull in left to clear the centre car. Total attention on driving. Watch the bend. Watch the hill. Watch the other driver. Note road works on left. Still quite a way to go before you actually pass him, but watch it. He might pull back in front of you. Perfect control. Perfect confidence. Recognition of 'Hazard' correctly allowed for. No danger.

Someone else on the road. Southbound vehicle coming towards you round the bend and over the hill. Crikey, he's shifting! But no danger, ample room for all three of us. But what's happening? That chap in the middle of the road is moving off. He's turning. He can't be, but he is.

Please, God, it can't be happening. It can't be true. They're going to hit.

'Foot off the gas. Cover the brake,' they'd said through all those months of training. So the brakes are already covered and those discs are earning their keep. The only emergency stop in a lifetime. And a stop so fast and so vicious that the imprint of the steering wheel is found in bruises on the body next morning. But even now it isn't your accident. Not yet. You've only stopped short because you know those two must hit and you are aiming to stay clear of that shambles. You have time to think. You have time to realise that they are going to hit and they will hit very hard, that you are the only one there to do what must be done and you are afraid. You are afraid of corpses and twisted metal and a steering column through the body and out of the back, and blood. You have time to be afraid of all that while they are busy hitting each other and your magnificent bit of machinery has brought itself to a dead stop, and far faster than any figures on the back of the Highway Code because these are discs in superb condition, and a good road, and four new tyres.

They do hit. You've underestimated the speed of the southbound vehicle. It goes head-on into the side of the car across its path, but that doesn't stop it. It doesn't even seem to slow it. It's coming on. It's out of control. It isn't even coming straight. It's crabwise and deformed, and as though some gigantic demon has picked it up and flung it; and it's coming for you – more or less. Your engine is still running. You've still got time. Your brain is still functioning. Left hand ditch? Can't. Roadworks. Swerve right? Can't. He might. And he's probably scattered bodies over there, anyway. Can't see because it's dark. Back? Only hope. Reduce impact. Instinct to glance in mirror. Nothing behind. Slam into reverse. Please God, let him miss. He's zig-zagging. He might miss. He must be still doing fifty. Clutch in. Just moving back. Reduce impact. Please God, NO!

Everyone has stopped. There are two people in your car now. There's you at the wheel, and there's you looking at you at the wheel. It's a funny sensation. You, at the wheel, you're a washout. You're in pain. You've never known such pain in all your life before. And you're moaning. Rather like a kitten, you're moaning, with quite regular mewing sounds. You're in a funny sort of position – you at the wheel, sort of twisted up. And you're not doing anything about it. You're just sitting there moaning. You, standing looking at you at the wheel, you're in better shape. You're saying: 'You've been in a crash, and you're probably the only person still alive. This is a main road, and other traffic will be coming along soon. That car on your bows has steam or smoke coming from under the bonnet. It is going to catch fire any second, and there are people in that car. You have got to get out. It doesn't matter how much you're hurt. You've got to get out. You've got to stop the traffic. You've got to see if there's anyone alive in there, and if there is, you've got to get them out.

The second you wins, and you find that you can get out, and you can walk. And the amazing thing is, there's a chap getting out of the car on your bonnet, and he can walk too, but he's all over bloody. And dirty. And he's clawing at his front passenger door because he's seen the smoke too. So you leave that to him, and you just concentrate on stopping the traffic, and you walk down the road towards a car. You're right in the middle of the road, and if he doesn't see you, or if he isn't quick enough off the mark, you're a goner, but you wave both hands at him and he stops. And you say: 'Please, there's been a terrible smash. It's just happened. You're the first here. There's people hurt. Killed, I think. Please go back and get an ambulance and the police. Please be quick. You can't go on. The road's blocked. Please be quick.' But he doesn't take it in. He wants to know what's happened, and whether there's room to turn round, and his window's jammed, and he hasn't the sense to open his door, and he's useless. But there's something else coming now, a heavy lorry. Sense from a lorry driver. Healthy young man, away at the double, and you go back.

And now the bloody young man is lifting a young girl from the wreckage and laying her on the verge among the roadworks. She is even bloodier than he is. You've still got one headlamp working, and that is the only light on the scene. You can see the blood quite clearly by the light of that lamp. She is writhing a bit on the verge, in an attitude of complete abandonment and indecency. Then she lies quite still and he covers her. You know she is dead. You wonder about the other car, but the young man is walking over there and you leave it to him again. Anyway, it's dark over there, and you're such a coward you don't want to go and look. You excuse yourself by thinking that as you know no first aid you could serve no useful purpose. So you stand beside what is left of your car, and you wait, and you don't look at the girl. And you don't really think about anything at all. You are not even in very great pain any more, but you know you've got to look at your right leg, because that's where the pain was, and you use the headlight to look, and it's all bloody and unreal-looking. That's YOUR leg. It's always been alright in the past. Best not look any more. That blood will just go away if you leave it.

For the first time in your life you are in an ambulance in a hurry. Lamps flashing, horns blowing, passing everything in sight. Wrong side of the road half the time. Magnificent driver. You have time to appreciate that. Beautiful driving, and everyone melting out of your road. The ambulance man explains that you are going straight to the city. Nearly 20 miles to go, but serious injuries aboard, and better to go straight to large teaching hospital. Moving very fast but very smooth. Young girl is lying on stretcher covered in blankets, face and head covered with blood-stained bandages. Blood is very light, bright sort of red, not the sort of colour you squeeze a drop of out of your finger. Apparently she's not dead, just very seriously injured. You know that, because the ambulance driver has radio as well, and he's telling the hospital all about all of you.

The boy who is so dirty and so bloody looks at you and says, 'Were you driving the second car I hit?' You say, 'Yes.' He says, 'You're my witness aren't you, that he pulled right across my path?' You say, 'Yes.' You want to add, 'But what the hell were you going at that speed for?' but you don't, because he has his arms round the girl who will soon be dead. And you look at the other chap – the good steady driver, the one you followed for miles, the one who made an atrocious error of judgement. You can't see much of him because of the bandages, but he doesn't say anything at all though his eyes are open. The ambulance attendant tries to talk to him but he doesn't answer, and the attendant tells the driver he doesn't like the look of him, and his head's in a mess, and for God's sake get a move on. You try not to look to your left. She is a middle-aged woman and there is so much blood on her you cannot tell where she is hurt. Why is the blood such a very light, bright red? She is being sick; she is very, very sick.

She goes on vomiting. And when she is not vomiting she is apologising, to you, and to the ambulance attendant, because you are being splashed with blood, or vomit, or whatever it is, and she is ashamed, and apologetic, and hurt, and helpless. And the attendant says, 'For God's sake get on with it, Tom. We've got a right load here.' And Tom says, 'Oh shut up!' And you say nothing.

The next day you are two lines in the National Press, and for about 4 days you are a paragraph in the local press. And now you are just statistics in the Road Accidents Report.

What do you think made that account dramatic?

Irene Read gave quite a clear, unjumbled version of what happened though she told it in a dramatic way. However, the next day, she had to give a statement to the police. For some of the people involved, a lot depended on her statement: prosecution, fines, loss of licence, possibly even imprisonment. She had to present her facts in as straightforward a manner as she could; and her tone would have been different from the account you read.

Work in groups of three or four. Read through the passage again and decide together on exactly what happened up until the point when Irene Read gets into the ambulance. You may find that drawing a sketch map will help. Then make some notes to help you with your statement to the police.

Choose a few people at random from the class to give their statements. The rest of the class should take the part of the police and feel free to ask any questions which would help clarify points which are obscure.

SECTION 2 WORKING IN GROUPS

Assignment 1 ## Deciding what to discuss

1·1

The event   Even quite simple events need to be planned well in advance. Working in groups of four or five, give yourselves 10 minutes to decide together what you should discuss in order to arrange one of the following activities.

1 Organising a lunchtime concert of live or recorded music in aid of a charity or of school funds.
2 Organising a sponsored walk, swim, bike ride, or eating/knitting/canoeing contest in aid of charity.
3 Arranging for a group of pupils to redecorate your classroom.
4 Preparing to take a group of handicapped young people for an afternoon outing.

Here's an example of a programme for discussion worked out by a group who planned to take a class of twenty-eight pupils and two teachers to Margate for the day:

Visit to Margate

1 Decide on date.
2 Find out costs of coach and rail fares. Reductions for party bookings?
3 Coach and train times?
4 Arrange time and place for meeting in the morning and in Margate for return.
5 Find out what attractions Margate has to offer.
6 Produce and distribute copies of instructions and of worksheet on Margate.
7 Get parents' permission for each member of the class.
8 Find out about insurance position.
9 Collect money from each person by certain date.

When you've finished your discussion, think about how well you worked as a group.

1 Did you complete your list in the time available?
2 Was there any disagreement? If so, how did you resolve it?
3 How did you organise yourselves? Did everyone join in? Did one person take over?
4 If the discussion came to a dead end, how did it get going again?
5 Did anyone get angry? If so, how do you think it could have been avoided?
6 How do you think you could have worked more successfully?
7 Would you have done better working as individuals?

Assignment 2 # Using an organiser

| 2·1 |

The jigsaw game   The purpose of this exercise is to show how an organiser can help or hinder work on a project.

What you need: *Four jigsaws (each of 100–200 pieces). Mix the pieces of two of the jigsaws together and put them on one side. Then do the same with the other two jigsaws.*

Form four groups of between five and eight people. Divide the class into four groups, A, B, C and D. Groups A and C have to separate the two jigsaws they are given and then complete both as far as they can in a time limit of 15 minutes.

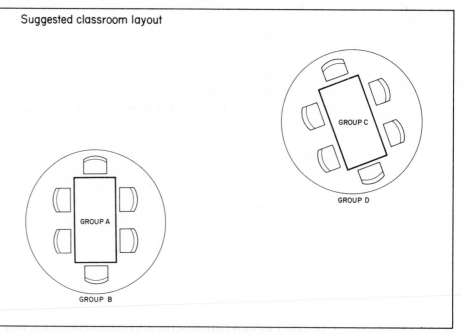

Suggested classroom layout

Groups B and D are Observer groups, B watching A and D watching C. Their task is to observe how well their jigsaw group is succeeding, using the questions given below.

Group A works without an organiser. Group C works with an organiser who should either be chosen by the teacher, elected in by group members, or chosen by lot. It's up to the group to decide.

The two pairs of groups should work as far away from each other as possible.

Here are some notes for the observer groups:

Observer groups – What to look for:

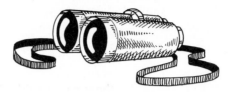

1 How did the organiser start things off? Did s/he think of asking for the picture of the jigsaws? How did s/he allocate the tasks which had to be done?
2 How did the group without an organiser start things off? Did anyone take the role of organiser?
3 What techniques did each group use to separate the two jigsaws?
4 Did they try to complete both jigsaws or only one?
5 How far did they get in their task?
6 Did everyone join in?
7 Were they working together as a team or did they get in each other's way?
8 Was there any argument? If so, how was it resolved?
9 In the group with an organiser, were the other members of the group co-operative?
10 If either group was successful, what do you think made it so?

When the jigsaw groups have had their 15 minutes, the observer groups should ask them questions about what happened. For example, 'Why did you decide to work in pairs?' They should also try to make constructive comments.

The observer groups B and D now try the exercise themselves. Each group should use the set of jigsaws and the method of working (i.e. with or without an organiser) which they did not observe in use. For example, group B would have the jigsaws previously used by group C. In their turn, the other groups can observe and comment on the way groups B and D perform their task.

2·2 What do you think you have learnt from this exercise:

1 about working with an organiser?
2 about observing?
3 about commenting tactfully on the way people work?
4 about learning from people's mistakes?

Assignment 3 **Using each person in a group**

3·1

The common room   The purpose of this exercise is to use each member of your group when planning the redecoration and equipment of a common room for fourth- and fifth-form pupils.

What you need: *Paint colour charts*
Furnishing, lighting and
vending machine
catalogues.

You should form groups of five to eight people. Assume you have fairly generous funds, but be realistic. Try to use an existing room in your school as your starting point. If possible, each group should go and look at the room together.

1 Each of you should contribute two suggestions, one for decoration and the other for furnishing, giving clear reasons for your choice.
2 You should discuss the various suggestions and then decide on a colour scheme and a list of suggested furnishings and equipment.
3 One of you should make notes on what the group decides are the best ideas.

4 You should draw up a simple plan, giving the positioning of major items of furniture, vending machines and so on.

5 One of you should present the group's ideas to the rest of the class.

6 The class should vote on which scheme they prefer.

N.B. Don't forget to find out if any of your group has got useful experience or knowledge. Has anyone recently had a room redecorated or helped redecorate it themselves? Has anyone got a particular interest in design or colour or furnishings? Which of you is studying art or CDT? Has anyone got relations or friends who might be useful?

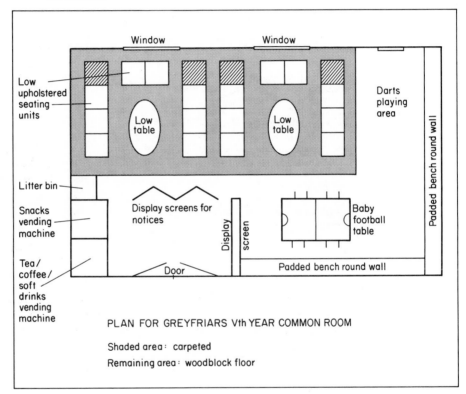

PLAN FOR GREYFRIARS Vth YEAR COMMON ROOM

Shaded area: carpeted

Remaining area: woodblock floor

Assignment 4 # Making decisions

| 4·1 | **Lost at sea** Work in groups of five to eight people. Imagine you are adrift on a private yacht in the South Pacific. As a result of a fire of unknown origin, much of the yacht and its contents have been destroyed. The yacht is now slowly sinking. Your location is not clear because you were all distracted trying to bring the fire under control. Your best estimate is that you are approximately 1000 miles south–southwest of the nearest land. |

Opposite is a list of fifteen items that are undamaged after the fire. In addition to these articles, you have a serviceable rubber life raft with oars which is large enough to carry the entire crew and all the items listed below. The total contents of all survivors pockets are a packet of cigarettes, several books of matches and five one-dollar bills.

Your task is to rank the fifteen items listed below in terms of their importance to your survival. Place the number 1 by the most important item, the number 2 by the second most important, and so on through to number 15, the least important.

Before you start, think about these points:

1 Do you want or need an organiser?
2 Are you going to vote on the order to place each item?
3 Think about a system for sorting the items into categories like 'VITAL'; 'USEFUL'; 'USELESS'.
4 Consider alternative uses for some of the items.
5 Find out how much time you have. This will affect how thoroughly you discuss each point.

When you've finished, you should be ready to give reasons for each of your decisions. If other groups have different ideas, you'll need to defend your decisions, so it's a good idea to think of arguments for the order in which you've placed each item.

Survival items

— — — — — — — — Sextant*
— — — — — — — — Shaving mirror
— — — — — — — — 5-gallon can of water
— — — — — — — — Mosquito netting
— — — — — — — — One case of army 'C' rations
— — — — — — — — Maps of the Pacific Ocean
— — — — — — — — Seat cushion (flotation device approved by coastguard)
— — — — — — — — 2-gallon can of oil–petrol mixture
— — — — — — — — Small transistor radio
— — — — — — — — Shark repellent
— — — — — — — — 20 square feet of opaque plastic
— — — — — — — — 1 quart of 160 proof Puerto Rican rum
— — — — — — — — 15 feet of nylon rope
— — — — — — — — Two boxes of chocolate bars
— — — — — — — — Fishing kit

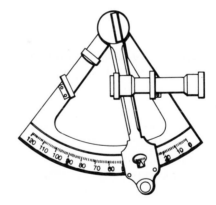

sextant – a navigational instrument for measuring latitude from the sun's elevation.

4·2

Survive the Savage Sea   It can be very important to make a group work well together and make the right decisions, but it's not often a matter of life and death. To one family, however, it was just that. The Robertson family decided they wanted a change from their life on a farm in North Staffordshire and planned a round the world voyage in a 43-foot schooner. In June 1972, after they had been on their voyage for 18 months, their yacht was sunk in the Pacific by killer whales. For 38 days, with few provisions, they survived in a small dinghy and a life raft at sea. The father,

Dougal, mother, Lyn (a nurse), son, Douglas (18), friend, Robin (22) and twin sons Neil and Sandy (13) managed to stay alive until they were eventually rescued by a Japanese fishing boat. Dougal Robertson later wrote a book, *Survive the Savage Sea* about their amazing adventures. Here are some extracts from it:

While the yacht was sinking, the family managed to launch their small dinghy, the Ednamair, *but as this was soon swamped with water, they all clambered into their inflatable life raft. They had with them a few salvaged odds and ends, a survival kit containing enough food and water for one person for 20 days, some flares and fishing tackle.*

First day

How long would this have to last us? We were over two hundred miles down wind and current from the Galapagos Islands. To try to row the small dinghy into two hundred miles of rough ocean weather was an impossible journey even if it was tried by only two of us in an attempt to seek help for the others left behind in the raft. The fact that the current was against us as well only put the seal of hopelessness on the idea. There was no way back.

Seventh day: the ship that didn't see them . . .

Douglas, lazily watching the dispersing clouds, suddenly sat up with a start, pointing excitedly. 'A ship! A ship! It's a ship!' We all crowded to the door of the raft, staring in the direction of his pointing finger; a cargo vessel of about six thousand tons was approaching us on a course that would bring her within three miles of us. I felt my heart pound against my ribs. 'Get out the flares,' I said hoarsely, 'and pass them to me in the dinghy, they'll see us better from there.'

Three miles was a fair distance, but on a dull day like this, against a background of rain they should see us easily. I clambered into the dinghy and Douglas passed me the rockets and hand flares; my hands trembled as a I ripped open a parachute rocket flare and, with a mute appeal to the thing to fire, struck the igniter on the fuse. It spluttered and hissed, then roared off on a trajectory high above the raft, its pinkish magnesium flare slowly spiralling downwards leaving a trail of smoke in the sky. They couldn't fail to see it. I waited a moment or two watching for the ship to alter course, then struck a hand flare, holding it high above my head. The blinding red light was hot to hold and I pointed it away from the wind to ease my hand, the red embers of the flare dropping into the dinghy; as it went out I struck another, smoke from the first now a rising plume in the sky; surely they must see that. I waited a little, my hands trembling. 'This chance might not come again,' I said, anxious faces crowding the door of the raft, 'I'm going to use our last rocket flare and one more hand flare.' We watched tensely as the second rocket flare soared and spiralled its gleaming distress message high above us; desperately I struck the third hand flare and held it high, standing on the thwart and holding on to the mast. 'Look, look, you bastards!' I shouted. 'Set fire to the sail!' Lyn's voice. I stuck the flare to the sail but it only melted. The ship sailed on slowly disappearing behind a rain shower, and when she reappeared her hull was half obscured by the horizon, five miles distant and disappearing fast. The time was eleven o'clock. My shoulders drooped. 'We daren't use another,' I said. 'They won't see it now and we have to keep something for the next one.' We had three hand flares left. Lyn smiled cheerfully. 'It says in the instruction book that the first one probably wouldn't see us,' she said slowly, 'and I'd already told the twins not to expect anything.' She gathered the twins to her, comfortingly. We stared at the dwindling speck on the horizon and felt so lonely that it hurt, 'I'm sorry lads,' I felt very tired. 'We used to consider that one of the most important tenets of good seamanship was "Keep a good lookout". That lot seem to be pretty poor seamen!' We would survive without them, yes, and that was the word from now on, 'survival', not 'rescue', or 'help', or dependence of any kind, just survival. I felt the strength flooding through me, lifting me from the depression of disappointment to a state of almost cheerful abandon. I felt the bitter aggression of the predator fill my mind. This was not our environment and the beasts around us would eat us if we failed. From that instant on, I became a savage.

Seventh day: the first turtle . . .

Towards late afternoon we felt an unusally hard bump on the raft floor, unlike the quick thrust of the striking dorado, and poking our heads out of the stern door of the raft we found ourselves gazing at the large scaly head of a turtle, protruding eyes set above a nasty-looking beak, surveying us with a dispassionate unblinking scrutiny. The day before I would have said, 'Leave it, we can't manage that,' but now things were different. 'We'll have this one,' I said. 'Let's get it aboard the dinghy.' The turtle's flippers had become entangled in the sea anchor line, so first passing a rope from the dinghy under the raft, we made it fast to one of the back flippers, then, carefully avoiding the searching beak, freed the turtle from the sea anchor rope and towed it around the raft to the *Ednamair*. I scrambled on to the dinghy and pulled the now struggling turtle alongside, reaching down to grasp the back flippers. I twisted the turtle round until its back was next to the dinghy and heaved. It was surprisingly heavy and as it came aboard, the dinghy tilted alarmingly. I threw my weight to the other side to trim her, then with a hump and a thrashing of claws the reptile lay on its back in the bottom of the dinghy, all eighty pounds of it. I put my thumbs up to the twins and Douglas watching from the raft, and they cheered excitedly.

Now for the difficult bit. I looked at the armoured amphibian with a farmer's eye; where to cut to reach the artery? I had helped to slaughter a few pigs and lambs and had a pretty good idea how to tackle this one. I grasped the pointed knife in my right hand and, putting a foot on each of the front flippers, held its beak with my left hand, then plunged the knife into the leathery skin of the neck, deep into the spinal column, then with quick, outward strokes of the knife to right and left I cut both vein and artery. Deep red blood spurted into the bottom of the dinghy and gradually, beak and flippers ceased thrashing as the beast died. Apart from a few minor scratches I was unscathed, so in the gathering dusk I washed the blood from my hands into the bottom of the dinghy, careful not to spill any in the water. I didn't want to bring any inquisitive sharks around, especially our hammerheaded friend, until we had started moving again, for if they suspected that the blood came from the raft they would probably attack the inflatable with disastrous consequences. Excitedly we discussed this addition to our larder. Lyn had heard from someone that turtle livers were inedible so we decided to discard the offal rather than risk illness. Twenty-four hours previously I would not have had the stomach for such a bloody business but the laws of survival applied and the first principle, 'The fittest survive, the weakest go to the wall', had now become our way of life. We would struggle and endure and if our reflexes were not as swift as the animals and fish around us, we had cunning, and we would improve with practice.

Thirty-sixth day: what they looked like . . .

Lyn washed and mended our clothes, which now had the appearance of some aboriginal garb. Douglas had only his shirt left (Lyn was trying to sew his shredded undershorts together in some attempt to make him presentable when we reached land); Lyn's housecoat, now in ribbons, was more ornament than use, and my tattered underpants and vest were stiff with turtle blood and fat. Robin and the twins were in rather better garb, for their labours made less demand on their clothing. I suppose we would have been thought a most indecent lot in civilised society. Robin and I had beards with unkempt moustaches which hung over our upper lips; salt water boils and scars covered our arms, legs and buttocks and were scattered on other parts of our anatomy, intermingled with claw-marks from turtles, as well as cuts and scratches from other sources. The adults were not desperately thin but the twins, Neil in particular, had become very emaciated. Knee cramps troubled us from time to time, but generally speaking, apart from Sandy who had a slight bronchial cough which Lyn's expert ear had detected the day previously (for she had a constant fear of a static pneumonia developing in our cramped situation), we were in better physical condition than when we had abandoned the raft.

Thirty-eighth day: rescue

I chopped up some dried turtle meat for tea, and Lyn put it with a little wet fish to soak in meat juice. She spread the dry sheets for the twins under the canopy, then prepared their little supper as we started to talk of Dougal's Kitchen and if it should have a wine licence. As we pondered the delights of Gaelic coffee, my eye, looking past the sail, caught sight of something that wasn't sea. I stopped talking and stared; the others all looked at me. 'A ship,' I said. 'There's a ship and it's coming towards us!' I could hardly believe it but it seemed solid enough. 'Keep still now!' In the sudden surge of excitement, everyone wanted to see. 'Trim her! We mustn't capsize now!' All sank back to their places.

I felt my voice tremble as I told them that I was going to stand on the thwart and hold a flare above the sail. They trimmed the dinghy as I stood on the thwart. 'Right, hand me a flare, and remember what happened with the last ship we saw!' They suddenly fell silent in memory of that terrible despondency when our signals has been unnoticed. 'Oh God!' prayed Lyn, 'please let them see us.' I could see the ship quite clearly now, a Japanese tunny fisher. Her grey and white paint stood out clearly against the dark cross swell. 'Like a great white bird,' Lyn said to the twins, and she would pass within about a mile of us at her nearest approach. I relayed the information as they listened excitedly, the tension of not knowing, of imminent rescue, building like a tangible, touchable, unbeatable unreality around me. My eye caught the outlines of two large sharks, a hundred yards to starboard. 'Watch the trim,' I warned. 'We have two man-eating sharks waiting if we capsize!' Then, 'I'm going to light the flare now, have the touch ready in case it doesn't work.'

I ripped the caps off; pulled the striker and struck the primer. The flare smoked then sparked into life, the red glare illuminating *Ednamair* and the sea around us in the twilight. I could feel my index finger roasting under the heat of the flare and waved it to and fro to escape the searing heat radiating outwards in the calm air, then unable to hear the beat any longer, I dropped my arm, nearly scorching Lyn's face, and threw the flare high in the air. It curved in a brilliant arc and dropped into the sea. 'Hand me another, I think she's altered course!' My voice was hoarse with pain and excitement and I felt sick with apprehension that it might only be the ship corkscrewing in the swell, for she had made no signal that she had seen us. The second flare didn't work. I cursed it in frustrated anguish as the priming substance chipped off instead of lighting. 'The torch!' I shouted, but it wasn't needed, she had seen us, and was coming towards us.

When you've read the extracts, think about the following questions:

1 If you were shipwrecked in a boat with a few others, what skills would you want them to have?
2 What kind of people would you like them to be?
3 What kind of people would you find most difficult to deal with?
4 Do you think it would help or hinder your chances of survival if the others were members of your family?
5 What do you think kept the Robertson family going?
6 The Robertson family had to eat raw meat and drink turtle blood in order to survive. Others in similar circumstances have even resorted to cannibalism. What would you be prepared to eat in order to survive?

4·3   **The Island Game**   Work in groups of five to eight people. A group of passengers has been shipwrecked. They clambered aboard a life raft when the large ship on which they were travelling sank in mid-Pacific. They have reached a small island, but have no idea where they are. There are no signs of other survivors from the ship.

THE SURVIVORS

Family of 4:
Mother – 41, area organiser for school meals.
Father – 40, dentist, with some general medical training
Twins – 14, one male, keen footballer; one female, winner of gymnastics medal.

The others:
Policewoman – 20, trained but inexperienced. Won the holiday on board ship in a competition.
Boiler stoker – 24, male, keen union member, doing a technology course with the Open University. Was working on board the ship.
Retired primary school teacher – 65, female, imaginative and creative. Has bad arthritis.
Docker – 42, male, unemployed for 2 years before getting a job as a deck hand on board ship.
Solicitor – 53, female, mother of two grown-up children (not present), recently divorced. Good clear thinker.
Professor of Sociology – 50, male, took early retirement as he didn't enjoy his job. Idealistic.
Boy – 16, separated from parents when the ship sank. The family were emigrating to Australia. He was doing a technology course at school. Has learnt some bricklaying.
Girl – 15, sister of boy described above. Has done a word-processing course. Is interested in dressmaking.
Boy – 16, travelling to visit uncle in Australia. Was in cadet corps at public school. Has done a survival course on Dartmoor.

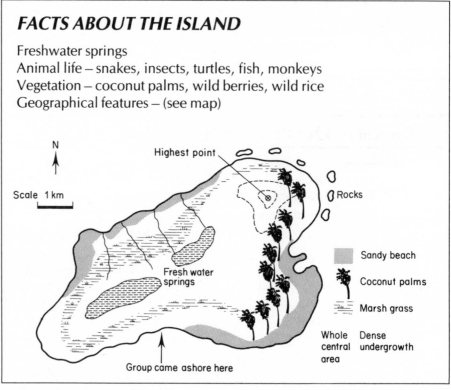

FACTS ABOUT THE ISLAND

Freshwater springs
Animal life – snakes, insects, turtles, fish, monkeys
Vegetation – coconut palms, wild berries, wild rice
Geographical features – (see map)

What you have to do:

1 Work out the main survival tasks for those on the island. Which are the most important?
2 Organise immediate action and allocate tasks to different members of the shipwrecked group.
3 Arrange long-term necessary activities and set up individuals and groups to work on particular problems. Who will be most suitable to do which job?
4 Do you see any problems arising from the groupings of people on the island? (For example, what are you going to do about the family? Suppose they want to go off on their own?) How will you deal with the problems you foresee?
5 What rules, if any, will you make for survival on the island? (For example, will you have a weekend or rest day? Will all food be shared exactly equally? And so on.)
6 How will you deal with people who break the rules? (For example, people who take too much food, don't do their jobs properly or at all, fight or quarrel with others, and so on.)

If you like, you could role play one or more of the incidents which you can imagine happening on the island.

SECTION 3

PEOPLE, PLACES AND EVENTS

Assignment 1 **Describing things**

1·1   **An old doll**   Here are two transcripts of people describing objects which have some meaning for them.

First, one girl talks about her old doll.

'Her name's Linda. I don't know why. I just liked the name. She was given to me when I was four. My nan thought I ought to have a proper doll. She had yellow hair which looked like it had been permed; all neat waves. I remember how it felt, sort of stiff and wiry. I thought she was beautiful. Of course she hasn't got any hair left. My brother pulled it all out one day to spite me. She hasn't got many clothes now, either. Just an old piece of red stuff my mum draped round her so she looked decent. But when I first got her she was so smart – she had a whole wardrobe full of clothes. You could collect them. I'm a bit ashamed to admit it, but she still sleeps in my bed at nights. I don't take her with me if I go away or anything like that; but I like it when she sits there waiting for me to come home.'

Here, a boy is talking about a pair of kitchen scales.

'It's not how I expected scales to be. I imagined them to be sort of like a see-saw, with ends which balanced and little weights you put on one side to tell how much there was on the other. That's what you expect scales to be like, isn't it? Anyway, this thing is just a plastic base with a bowl that fits over the top like a hat. You turn the bowl the other way up when you want to weigh something. On the bottom bit there's a scale marked out in pounds and kilos. It's got spiky little lines shooting up and a green indicator light which goes on over the top of the line when you've weighed whatever it is. Do you see what I mean? In a few years time I bet there'll be this stupid computer voice announcing how many pounds or grams of flour you've measured out. And then it'll probably try to tell you it's not enough for the recipe you've programmed in. I hate that kind of bossy machine. If I ever have to own a pair of kitchen scales I'll go right out and get one of the old-fashioned sort. With those neat little weights I was telling you about.'

31

Do you think these descriptions are successful? If you do, what do you think it is that makes them work? What other ways are there of making a description of a very ordinary thing come to life?

Think of a fairly ordinary object that has some meaning for you, either because you have some good or bad memories attached to it, or because you have some opinion about it, or because you think it's particularly beautiful or ugly, or for any other reason. Before you start working on your description, think about whether describing its colour or shape or smell or taste or sound or texture will help your listeners to be interested. And remember that in this kind of description, talking about what it means to you personally is what is most likely to gain your audience's attention. When you've got some ideas, work in pairs or groups or as a class and try out your descriptions on your audience.

Assignment 2 **Describing places**

2·1 **Five senses** Look at these photographs of different places:

Working either as a whole class or in small groups, decide on your answers to these questions, applying them to only one of the photographs:

1 What do you think would be the main colours used in your picture if it wasn't in black and white?
2 Think of six adjectives to describe your picture.
3 The five senses are sight, sound, touch, taste and smell. What do you think you might see, hear, touch, taste and smell if you were inside your picture? For example, in picture 4 you might see some furry brown calves, hear hens scratching in the yard, feel the rough wood of a fence, smell manure or silage and taste the stalk of a buttercup you picked along the way.
4 Individually, think of experiences you associate with one or more of the pictures. Can you remember how you felt, what you ate, what you saw and heard in similar places or on similar occasions? Try to describe what you remember to the others.

2·2 **Describing a visit**   Choose one of the photographs and think about how you would talk about a visit to a similar place. For example, if you chose photograph 3 you might decide to talk about the time you went to a particular football match. In that case you could describe what you remember about the sights, smells, sounds and so on, as well as any incidents that happened on that occasion. Each person in the class could then record a description or talk about it to the rest of the class.

Assignment 3 **Describing people**

| 3·1 |

Types of people
1 What does a bank manager look like?
2 Describe a 'typical' mother.
3 What sort of person becomes a teacher?
4 Which of your friends would make a good supervisor in a big store?
5 What qualities does a salesman or saleswoman need?
6 If you had to employ someone to look after a baby, what sort of person would you look for?
7 What makes the perfect DJ?
8 What sort of person becomes a policeman or woman?
9 Describe a small-time criminal.

How did you come to these conclusions?
From your own experience?
From TV programmes or adverts?
From what you've heard other people say?

| 3·2 |

Describing character
1 Here are some different ways people used to describe character in the past:

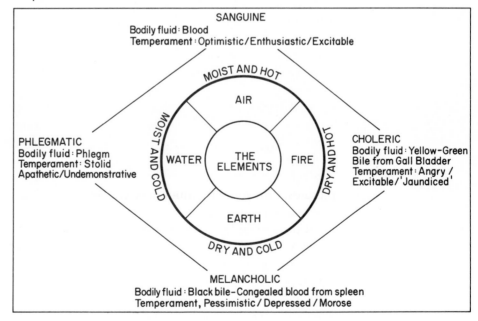

Can you think of people you know or characters on television who would fit each of these humours?

Aries
March 21 to April 20

The Ram. A fire sign, ruled by Mars. Loves a challenge and an adventure. Impulsive and headstrong; pioneering, full of initiative.

Taurus
April 21 to May 22

The Bull. An earth sign, ruled by Venus. Patient – as a rule! Loves beauty, art and comfort. Determined, and works hard.

Gemini
May 23 to June 21

The Twins. An air sign, ruled by Mercury. Quick and lively, enjoying all communication and contact with other people. Full of curiosity.

Cancer
June 22 to July 22

The Crab. A water sign, ruled by the moon. Secretive and sensitive. Motherly, and protective of those who are weaker. Moody and imaginative.

Leo
July 23 to August 22

The Lion. A fire sign, ruled by the sun. Likes to be at the centre of attention and activity; creative, and a lover of life. Generous but authoritarian.

Virgo
August 23 to September 22

The Maiden who cuts the corn. An earth sign, ruled by Mercury. Precise, careful in work and very conscientious. Likes to do everything thoroughly, and is interested in matters of health.

Libra
September 23 to October 22

The Scales. An air sign, ruled by Venus. Weighs matters up, and considers carefully before taking action. Likes co-operation and getting on well with other people.

Scorpio
October 23 to November 21

The Scorpion. A water sign, ruled by Mars and Pluto. Passionate and intense. Loyal, ruthless – an 'all or nothing' person.

Sagittarius
November 22 to December 22

The Archer. A fire sign, ruled by Jupiter. Loves freedom, space; is very enthusiastic. Humorous, but often a tease.

Capricorn
December 23 to January 20

The Goat. An earth sign, ruled by Saturn. Serious-minded, ambitious, and prudent. Will climb to the top of the mountain even if it takes a lifetime.

Aquarius
January 21 to February 19

The Watercarrier. An air sign, ruled by Saturn and Uranus. Highly individualistic, often unconventional and wilful. A lover of truth; interested in other people and cultures.

Pisces
February 20 to March 20

The Fish. A water sign, ruled by Jupiter and Neptune. Emotional and impressionable. Very changeable according to environment. Artistic, idealistic and 'other worldly'.

Do you think these are good descriptions of 12 different types of people?
If you're honest, do you think your sun sign describes you accurately?

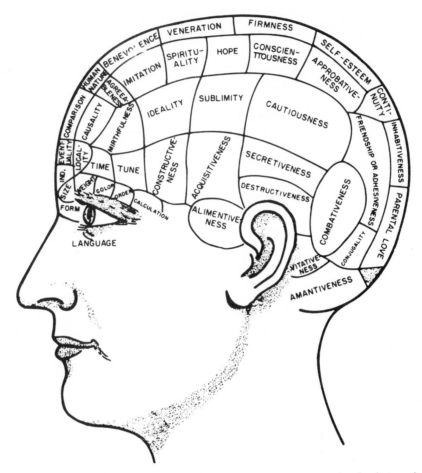

Phrenology – 18th and 19th century: pseudo-science which claimed to allow personality to be assessed by feeling the bumps on the head. A big bump in a particular place could be interpreted as a strength in the quality supposed to be sited there.

2 Imagine that you have to make notes for a character reference for your best friend or an enemy or someone you admire. It should be someone you know well. You should be absolutely honest as no job or future prospect depends on what you say. Obviously you shouldn't give the name of the person.

Try to include comments under these headings:

Appearance	– (smart, untidy, kind of clothes worn, hairstyle, etc.)
Reliability	– (punctual, lets you know if going to be late or missing; does what s/he promises, etc.)
Strengths	– (what s/he is good at)
Weaknesses	– (what s/he is not so good at)
Personal qualities	– (sympathetic, kind, friendly, mean, aggressive, etc.)

Think of incidents to illustrate what you say. For example, if s/he has or has not let you down when you've been going out; times when s/he has shown aggression or sympathy and so on.

Be ready to use your notes to talk about the person, either to a small group or the whole class.

3 Working with a partner, you could prepare a description of your own character using the headings suggested on page 37.

3·3 **Describing appearance** Each person in the class should make notes for a physical description of a person they know well, using the following headings as a guide:

Build	(tall, short, thin, thick-set, long or short legs)
Face	(most noticeable features – e.g. big nose, large eyes, small mouth, colouring, facial hair, spectacles)
Hair	(colour, style)
Walk	(fast, slow, head bent, straight neck or back)
Mannerisms	(use of gestures when speaking, etc.)
Speech	(talkative or silent, speaks fast or slowly, accent)
Dress	(usual style of clothing worn, colours, fashion conscious)

Assignment 4 **Describing incidents**

4·1 **Hit and run** Divide into groups of four or five people. Only one person in each group should look at the illustrations below and opposite.

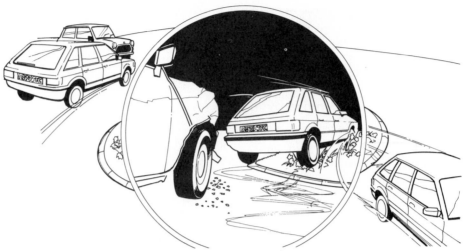

The person who has studied the illustrations should now tell one other person in the group what happened from the point of view of the cyclist. The second person should tell another member of the group and so on until the last person has heard the story. S/he should then explain what has happened as clearly as possible. This version should then be checked against the illustration to see how far the story has changed from the original. It is important that only the first member of the group is able to study the illustration in detail.

4·2   **Snatch and grab**   Work in groups of three or four. Look carefully at the story line illustrated below and overleaf.

1 Each person in the group should imagine him/herself in one of the
  following roles:
   (a) The checkout assistant who was robbed.
   (b) A security guard who chased the boy on roller skates.
   (c) A customer standing near the till that was robbed.
   (d) The checkout assistant at the next till.
   The police have just arrived and you are all standing around waiting to
   see what will happen. Talk about the incident together, describing what
   each of you saw, how you felt and what you did. Add any details you
   think relevant. You should also discuss your theories about what
   happened – was it a coincidence or was it planned? What could have
   been done to prevent it? And so on. Try to make your conversation as
   realistic as possible.

2 Your local radio station wants to interview people about the incident.
  Take it in turns to be the reporter who wants a lively interview for a
  news programme. Each of you should then be interviewed about what
  happened, keeping the roles you played in 1.

Assignment 5	**Telling a story**

5·1   **A scene from my autobiography**   Think of something that's happened in your life that might interest other people. It doesn't have to be particularly exciting or dramatic; it could be quite an ordinary event like a first trip on a train or aeroplane, or a stay in hospital when you were a child, or a performance in a school play or a time when you were lost or scared.

Here's a transcript of an account of what happened when a party of young people from a school in the middle of a city went on holiday in the Lake District.

'It was so dark that when he turned off the lights in the mini bus and we got out you couldn't see anything at all. And I mean nothing. Not even your hand in front of your face. Just sounds. Water and leaves and this funny rustling noise. I was so scared I hung on to the sleeve of the bloke next to me. No one said anything for what seemed like ages. Then something barged into me. I think I yelled. Anyway, that set everyone else off. We ended up all clinging together for dear life. One of the girls had hold of my arm and was digging her nails right in. I could still see the marks a week later. I think some people were actually crying. It turned out later that it had been a sheep, but I wasn't to know that at the time. This teacher had the idea that we were all poor little city boys and girls and we ought to find out what the country was really like. So he took us up to stay in this youth hostel miles away from anywhere and on the second night we were there he pushed us all into the mini bus and took us up on top of some mountain, made us get out, switched off all the lights and told us to shut up. There was no moon or anything. I don't think I've ever been so frightened in my whole life.'

What do you think made that account work? Did you get some sense of what it must have been like to be there at the time? How could the speaker have made what he had to say more dramatic?

Did you notice that whatever you may think of his account, he did at least focus on the one incident. It's usually better to start straight away on the main part of your story; you can lose your listeners' attention if you start with a long introduction about how you came to be in that situation in the first place. You notice that he didn't talk about the teacher's plan until he was halfway through his story.

When you've chosen the incident you're going to talk about, think how you will arrange your story so as to make it as interesting as possible. You could use the points listed overleaf to help with your plan.

1 Start with a dramatic opening that will gain your listeners' attention.
   This might be something that happened in the middle of the experience
   you're going to talk about. You can then flashback to what led up to that
   moment. Don't, in any case, go on too long with the preliminaries.
   People are mainly interested in the things which actually happened.
2 Give some atmospheric background to help the others identify with
   what is happening and with what you were feeling. For example, it
   helps if you can say what a place looks like, what sounds and smells
   there were – to a child in hospital, the smell of disinfectant may be very
   noticeable, and the doctors and nurses may seem very big and
   frightening.
3 Don't include too many characters; it is confusing and takes your
   listeners away from the main focus of the story, which is what happened
   to you and how you felt about it.
4 Try to end in a definite way; don't just say something like, 'well that was
   about all, really . . .' Try to think of a comment which will round the
   whole thing off. For example, the story of the child in hospital might end
   something like this: 'When the time came to go home, I almost didn't
   want to leave. I've never forgotten that teddy bear.'

When you've planned your story, tell it to the rest of the class or the other
members of a small group.

5·2 **Asking for more information** While you listen to each story, think of any
questions you could ask about what happened which would either clear
up something you didn't quite understand, or give other information about
the background to the story or help the speaker if s/he gets stuck at any
point. However, you should try not to interrupt if the story is going well,
but save your questions until the end.

SECTION 4 CONVERSATION

Assignment 1 **Encouraging a response**

1·1

Interviewing   Work in pairs, with one person acting as the Interviewer (A) and the other as the Interviewee (B).

A interviews B for 2 minutes on any subject. For example, you could talk about what s/he did last weekend; holidays; TV programmes and so on.

B should sit quite still, looking at the floor and answering the questions in a monotonous voice.

At the end of the 2 minutes, all the As should talk about how they felt the interview went and collect a list of comments. The Bs should do the same.

Now change partners so that you are talking to someone new *and* taking the other role: i.e. if you were an A before, you are now a B and vice versa.

The As should interview Bs as before for 2 minutes. This time, Bs should still look at the floor, but may speak in a normal, animated tone of voice.

Compare notes as after the first part of the exercise and note any differences in the responses from both As and Bs. Was it easier or harder to get and give information this time?

Change partners and roles again. This time Bs can relax and respond as they like.

Again, compare notes and discuss the differences between your experiences in this interview and the earlier ones.

Discuss the whole exercise.

What do you think was the effect of the three different styles of answering?

What is the value of body language, especially eye contact?

What is the value of varying your tones of voice?

Which kinds of questions did you find most effective in getting a good response?

Did you use questions which followed up answers given by the interviewee, even if they weren't questions you had originally planned to ask?

Work in pairs. As before, the interviewer, A, should ask the interviewee, B, about any ordinary subject, for example, an average day's events. This time, B should only answer the exact question asked. For example, if you're asked if you enjoy breakfast, the answer should probably be 'yes', 'no' or 'sometimes', with no explanation as to what kind of breakfast you like or if you prefer to eat it in bed or with the radio on and so on. It is then up to the interviewer to get other information from you. You should not try to be deliberately unhelpful, but just to take the questions as meaning exactly what they say. The interviewer should be careful not to ask questions which can only have a 'yes' or 'no' answer. It's better to say something like 'What sort of thing do you have for breakfast?' than 'Do you like toast?'. If your interviewee answers 'Eggs and stuff, you know,' you can follow up by saying 'What kind of stuff?' and so on.

1·2 **Pursuing the story**   Work in pairs. Imagine you are taking part in a chat show which specialises in talking to people about important, amusing, embarrassing or fascinating moments in their lives. There is a well-known presenter who asks the questions, which are designed to extract as much information as possible from those who agree to take part.

Here's a transcript of a typical interview from the show.

WALTER: Good evening, and welcome to the Walter Nago show.
(APPLAUSE) Our visitor tonight is Jim Daley who lives in Devon.
Hello, Jim.

JIM: Hello.

WALTER: Can you tell us what you do, Jim?

JIM: I'm a driving instructor.

WALTER: A driving instructor. Dangerous job, that, Jim.

JIM: Oh, not really. Pretty safe, these days, with dual controls.

WALTER: But there must be times when it isn't quite so safe, eh, Jim?

JIM: Oh, I don't know.

WALTER: Don't you ever get people who make you just a teeny weeny bit frightened, Jim? Just sometimes you must wish you'd gone into some nice safe job – deep sea diving, for instance? (LAUGHTER)

JIM: No, I can't say I've ever wished that.

WALTER: But didn't you once have a pupil who was, let's put it politely, just a little past the best age for learning to drive?

JIM: Well, I did have one man. (PAUSE)

WALTER: Yes, he was a pensioner, wasn't he?

JIM: I think he was about 75. Or perhaps it was 85 . . . It was a long time ago, you know.

WALTER: What sort of things did this 85-year-old man do that made you so frightened, eh Jim?

JIM: Well, there was one time . . . He had difficulties starting the car, see, and if he did manage it he used to go charging off down the road at about 40 miles an hour. One time he hit four other cars in the space of 100 yards. One of them was a Rolls. Real smart flashy job, open topped. He made a right mess of that one.

WALTER: I bet the owner was a bit annoyed, wasn't he?

JIM: I'll say. He was a wrestler. Huge great chap. Came out of his house, walked over to our car, tipped it over onto the side and kicked in the back window. Then there was another time when this same old guy thought he'd break the land speed record along the sands at Exmouth. That was really funny. (LAUGHS)

WALTER: What happened?

JIM: Oh, he drove into the sea and nearly drowned himself.
(PROLONGED LAUGHTER AND APPLAUSE)

How did Walter manage to get Jim to tell his story?

Working with your partner, think of a funny, interesting or embarrassing incident that one of you can remember. Then role play a television interview where one of you acts as the interviewer and the other as the guest, invited along to tell the story. The interviewer should ask questions so that the incident is told in a lively and interesting way. You could either act out the result for the rest of the class or record it on tape or video.

1·3   **Provoking a response**   You are working as a reporter for a new consumer programme which investigates the public response to unusual new ideas for products. Your job is to interview members of the public about these ideas and to come back with some kind of amusing or hostile or enthusiastic response.

Choose one or more of the products listed below (or think of your own ideas) and interview as many people as possible to find out their opinions.

New products

A magazine featuring articles of special interest for young people of both sexes.

A TV series on current events aimed at the 15–18 age group.

A range of make-up for the macho man.

A new soft drink for adults which contains low alcohol wine, no added sugar and fruit juice.

A range of unusual frozen foods including frogs' legs, worm protein in tomato sauce, locusts in batter and so on.

A miniature portable TV which can be attached to a new sort of headgear.

Edible cutlery for use at parties, on air flights etc.

Before you start, plan a list of questions which you can use to prompt the people you talk to. For example, you could mention the need for portable TV on long journeys, when commuting to work, for pillion passengers on motorbikes and so on. Macho make-up might look particularly good on football stars, wrestlers and boxers. You could mention the strong man film stars who certainly wear it, at least on film. Edible cutlery might be very popular at children's tea parties. Try to think of ways to make your interviewee respond, don't just stick to the 'what do you think of . . .' kind of question.

When you've finished your interviews, report back to the rest of the class on some of the reactions you got. You should have taken notes of the best answers or even used a tape recorder.

Assignment 2 **Carrying on talking (Bookshelf)**

2.1 **Different kinds of books** Read these extracts from four different types of books.

a The big tires sang a high note on the pavement. Joad's dark quiet eyes became amused as he stared along the road. The driver waited and glanced uneasily over. At last Joad's long upper lip grinned up from his teeth and he chuckled silently, his chest jerked with the chuckles. 'You sure took a hell of a long time to get to it, buddy.'

The driver did not look over. 'Get to what? How do you mean?'

Joad's lip stretched tight over his long teeth for a moment, and he licked his lips like a dog, two licks, one in each direction from the middle. His voice became harsh. 'You know what I mean. You give me a goin'-over when I first got in. I seen you.' The driver looked straight ahead, gripped the wheel so tightly that the pads of his palms bulged, and the backs of his hands paled. Joad continued, 'You know where I come from.' The driver was silent. 'Don't you?' Joad insisted.

'Well—sure. That is—maybe. But it ain't none of my business. I mind my own yard. It ain't nothing to me.' The words tumbled out now. 'I don't stick my nose in nobody's business.' And suddenly he was silent and waiting. And his hands were still white on the wheel. A grasshopper flipped through the window and lighted on top of the instrument panel, where it sat and began to scrape its wings with its angled jumping legs. Joad reached forward and crushed its hard skull-like head with his fingers, and he let it into the wind stream out the window. Joad chuckled again while he brushed the bits of broken insect from his fingertips. 'You got me wrong, mister,' he said. 'I ain't keepin' quiet about it. Sure I been in McAlester. Been there four years. Sure these is the clothes they give me when I come out. I don't give a damn who knows it. An' I'm goin' to my old man's place so I don't have to lie to get a job.'

The driver said, 'Well—that ain't none of my business. I ain't a nosy guy.'

'The hell you ain't,' said Joad. 'That big old nose of yours been stickin' out eight miles ahead of your face. You had that big nose goin' over me like a sheep in a vegetable patch.'

The driver's face tightened. 'You got me all wrong—' he began weakly.

Joad laughed at him. 'You been a good guy. You give me a lift. Well, hell! I done time. So what! You want to know what I done time for, don't you?'

'That ain't none of my affair.'

'Nothin' ain't none of your affair except skinnin' this here bull-bitch along, an' that's the least thing you work at. Now look. See that road up ahead?'

'Yeah.'

'Well, I get off there. Sure, I know you're wettin' your pants to know what I done. I ain't a guy to let you down.' The high hum of the motor dulled and the song of the tires dropped in pitch. Joad got out his pint and took another short drink. The truck drifted to a stop where a dirt road opened at right angles to the highway. Joad got out and stood beside the cab window. The vertical exhaust pipe puttered up its barely visible blue smoke. Joad leaned toward the driver. 'Homicide,' he said quickly. 'That's a big word—means I killed a guy. Seven years. I'm sprung in four for keepin' my nose clean.'

The driver's eyes slipped over Joad's face to memorize it. 'I never asked you nothin' about it,' he said. 'I mind my own yard.'

'You can tell about it in every joint from here to Texola.' He smiled. 'So long, fella. You been a good guy. But look, when you been in stir a little while, you can smell a question comin' from hell to breakfast. You telegraphed yours the first time you opened your trap.' He patted the metal door with the palm of his hand. 'Thanks for the lift,' he said. 'So long.' He turned away and walked into the dirt road.

For a moment the driver stared after him, and then he called, 'Luck!' Joad waved his hand without looking around. Then the motor roared up and the gears clicked and the great red truck rolled heavily away.

b

Wood tapped sharply on the gong. I waited on my toes, to see if he would come straight in, like a Hellene, and grab me round the body. No; I had guessed right. He was edging round, trying to get the sun in my eyes. He did not fidget on his feet, but moved quite slowly and softly, like a cat before it springs. Not for nothing I had felt, while he spoke bad Greek, that we yet had a common language. Now we spoke it. He, too, was a wrestler who thought.

His eyes were golden brown, light like a wolf's. 'Yes,' I thought 'and he will be as fast. Let him come in first; if he is going to take a risk, he will do it then. Afterwards he may know better.'

He aimed a great buffet at my head. It was meant to sway me left; so I jumped right. That was well, for where my guts should have been he landed a kick like a horse's. Even glancing it hurt, but not too much, and I grabbed his leg. As I tipped him over I jumped at him, throwing him sideways and trying to land on him with a head-lock. But he was fast, fast as a cat. He got me by the foot and turned my fall, and almost before I had touched ground was slipping round to get a scissors on me. I jabbed my fist at his chin, and saved myself by a lizard's tail-flick. Then the mill on the ground began in earnest. I soon forgot I had been slow to anger; you cease to ask what wrong a man has done you, when his hands are feeling for your life.

He had the look of a gentleman. But the Queen's stare had warned

me, when I asked the rules. All-in is all-in among the Shore People, and nothing barred. This slit in my ear like a fighting dog's, I got in that fight as a dog gets it. Once he nearly gouged out my eye, and only gave over to keep his thumb unbroken. Soon I got too angry rather than too cold; but I could not afford to take a risk, just for the pleasure of hurting him. He was like tanned ox-hide with a core of bronze.

As we twisted and kicked and struck, I could make believe no longer I was nineteen. I was fighting a man in his flower of strength, before I had come to mine. My blood and bones began to whisper he would outstay me. Then the gong began.

c

'So you tell me that you have never kissed anyone?' he said. He had a way of looking at me that made me feel innocent. He was staring now. Sometimes directly into my pupils, other times his eyes would roam all over my face and settled for a minute on my neck. My neck. My neck was snow-white and I was wearing a silk dress with a curved neckline. It was an ice-blue dress with blossoms on it. Sometimes I thought they were tiny apple blossoms and then again I thought the pattern was one of snow falling; but either way it was a nice dress and the skirt was composed of millions of little pieces that flowed when I walked.

'The next time we have lunch, don't wear lipstick,' he said. 'I prefer you without it.'

The coffee was bitter. I used four lumps of sugar. We came out and went to the pictures. He bought me a box of chocolates with a ribbon on it.

I cried halfway through the picture because there was a sad bit about a boy having to leave a girl in order to go off to war. He laughed when he saw me crying and whispered that we should go out. He took my hand as we went up the dark passage, and out in the vestibule he wiped my eyes and told me to smile.

We drove home while it was still bright. The hills in the distance were blue and the trees in the folds of the hills were a dusty lilac. Farmers were saving hay in fields along the roadside and children were sitting on haycocks eating apples and throwing butts over the ditch. The smell of hay came through the window, half spice, half perfume.

A woman wearing wellingtons was driving cows home to be milked. We had to slow down to let them in a side gate and I caught him looking at me. We smiled at each other and his hand came off the steering-wheel and rested on the lap of my ice-blue dress. My hand was waiting for it. We locked our fingers and for the rest of the journey we drove like that, except going round sharp bends. His hand was small and white and very smooth. There were no hairs on it.

'You're the sweetest thing that ever happened to me,' he said. It was all he said and it was only a whisper. Afterwards, lying in bed in the convent, I used to wonder whether he said it or whether I had imagined it.

He squeezed my hand before I got out of the car. I thanked him and reached into the back seat for my packages. He sighed, as if he were going to say something; but Baba ran out to the car and he slipped away from me.

My soul was alive; enchantment; something I had never known before. It was the happiest day of my whole life.

'Good-bye, Mr Gentleman,' I said through the window. There was an odd expression in his smile which seemed to be saying, 'Don't go.' But he did go, my new god, with a face carved out of pale marble and eyes that made me sad for every woman who hadn't known him.

'What'n the hell are you mooning about?' Baba asked, and I went into the house laughing.

'I bought you a present,' I said, and in my mind I kept singing it, 'You're the sweetest thing that ever happened to me.' It was like having a precious stone in my pocket and I had only to say the words in order to feel it, blue, precious, enchanting ... my deathless, deathless song.

d

In the corner, the robot's head swung up sharply, but then wobbled about imperceptibly. It pulled itself up to its feet as if it was about five pounds heavier than it actually was, and made what an outside observer would have thought was a heroic effort to cross the room. It stopped in front of Trillian and seemed to stare through her left shoulder.

'I think you ought to know I'm feeling very depressed,' it said. Its voice was low and hopeless.

'Oh God,' muttered Zaphod and slumped into a seat.

'Well,' said Trillian in a bright compassionate tone, 'here's something to occupy you and keep your mind off things.'

'It won't work,' droned Marvin, 'I have an exceptionally large mind.'

'Marvin!' warned Trillian.

'Alright,' said Marvin, 'what do you want me to do?'

'Go down to number two entry bay and bring the two aliens up here under surveillance.'

With a microsecond pause, and a finely calculated micromodulation of pitch and timbre – nothing you could actually take offence at – Marvin managed to convey his utter contempt and horror of all things human.

'Just that?' he said.

'Yes,' said Trillian firmly.

'I won't enjoy it.' said Marvin.

Zaphod leapt out of his seat.

'She's not asking you to enjoy it,' he shouted, 'just do it will you?'

'Alright,' said Marvin like the tolling of a great cracked bell, 'I'll do it.'

'Good . . .' snapped Zaphod, 'great . . . thank you . . .'

Marvin turned and lifted his flat-topped triangular red eyes up towards him'.

'I'm not getting you down at all am I?' he said pathetically.

'No no Marvin,' lilted Trillian, 'that's just fine, really . . .'

'I wouldn't like to think I was getting you down.'

'No, don't worry about that,' the lilt continued, 'you just act as comes naturally and everything will be just fine.'

'You're sure you don't mind?' probed Marvin.

'No, no Marvin,' lilted Trillian, 'that's just fine, really . . .' just part of life.'

Marvin flashed him an electronic look.

'Life,' said Marvin, 'don't talk to me about life.'

He turned hopelessly on his heel and lugged himself out of the cabin. With a satisfied hum and a click the door closed behind him.

'I don't think I can stand that robot much longer Zaphod,' growled Trillian.

Working either in small groups or as a class. discuss what you think of the extracts. You could use the following questions as a guide.

1 Would you want to read any of the books? What kind of details interested you? What put you off ?
2 What do you think each of the books might be about?
3 What do you think might happen next in each case?
4 What might have happened up to this point in the story?
5 Devise a plot which might include the incident in the extract.
6 Is there a particular type of book which would interest girls more than boys and vice versa? Why?
7 Have any of you read any similar type of books?

2·2   **Now read on**   Work in groups of about four or five. Each of you should bring in an extract from a book you've enjoyed reading. You should either read it aloud yourself or ask someone else to do so. Then,

1 Explain why you liked it.
2 Give a brief summary of what happens in the story.
3 Say what you found interesting about the main characters. Try to describe them, either in your own words or using short extracts from the book.
4 Where is the story set?
5 What was the ending like? Did you find it satisfying or unsatisfying?
6 What sort of book is it? Exciting, romantic, full of suspense, funny, escapist or like real life?
7 See if you can make the others want to read it. On page 54 are two examples of 'blurbs'. One is taken from the back of a book called *Little Sisters* by Fay Weldon and the other from *Spy Story* by Len Deighton. The publishers have tried to whet the reader's appetite by making them sound exciting and interesting. Work out a spoken version of a 'blurb' for the book you have chosen.

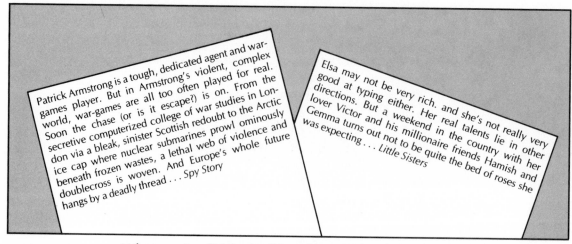

Patrick Armstrong is a tough, dedicated agent and war-games player. But in Armstrong's violent, complex world, war-games are all too often played for real. Soon the chase (or is it escape?) is on. From the secretive computerized college of war studies in London via a bleak, sinister Scottish redoubt to the Arctic ice cap where nuclear submarines prowl ominously beneath frozen wastes, a lethal web of violence and doublecross is woven. And Europe's whole future hangs by a deadly thread . . . *Spy Story*

Elsa may not be very rich. and she's not really very good at typing either. Her real talents lie in other directions. But a weekend in the country with her lover Victor and his millionaire friends Hamish and Gemma turns out not to be quite the bed of roses she was expecting . . . *Little Sisters*

When you've finished talking about the book, read the extract you've chosen again and find out from the others what they liked and disliked about what you've read. Try to ask specific questions rather than just a vague, 'well, did you like it then?' Find out if anyone else has read this or a similar book. Is there any prejudice against the sort of book you've been discussing? For example, do some people react to a romantic story by saying 'It's so boring,' or to a thriller by saying 'It's too violent'. Is there any way of persuading them of the opposite point of view? Try to keep the discussion going for at least 5 minutes. Plan your questions before you start.

After you've discussed the various extracts, decide on a list of ten books that the members of your class have most enjoyed. You'll find below a list of the ten most popular novels read by young people in one particular school. How does your list compare with it?

TOP TEN LIST

The Secret Diary of Adrian Mole Aged 13¾ – Sue Townsend
The Growing Pains of Adrian Mole – Sue Townsend
Animal Farm – George Orwell
The Hobbit – J. R. Tolkien
Lord of the Rings – J. R. Tolkien
To Kill a Mockingbird – Harper Lee
Nineteen Eighty-Four – George Orwell
Flowers in the Attic – Virginia Andrews
The Clockwork Orange – Anthony Burgess
The Hitchhiker's Guide to the Galaxy – Douglas Adams

2·3   **Bestsellers**

1 Some authors say that it is possible to write a book which is sure to be a bestseller. What do you think are the ingredients for a bestselling book? Here is an extract from *The Secret Diary of Adrian Mole Aged 13¾*. Why do you think it became a bestseller?

Thursday   January 1st
BANK HOLIDAY IN ENGLAND, IRELAND, SCOTLAND AND WALES

These are my New Year's resolutions:

1. I will help the blind across the road.
2. I will hang my trousers up.
3. I will put the sleeves back on my records.
4. I will not start smoking.
5. I will stop squeezing my spots.
6. I will be kind to the dog.
7. I will help the poor and ignorant.
8. After hearing the disgusting noises from downstairs last night, I have also vowed never to drink alcohol.

   My father got the dog drunk on cherry brandy at the party last night. If the RSPCA hear about it he could get done. Eight days have gone by since Christmas Day but my mother still hasn't worn the green lurex apron I bought her for Christmas! She will get bathcubes next year.
   Just my luck, I've got a spot on my chin for the first day of the New Year!

Friday   January 2nd
BANK HOLIDAY IN SCOTLAND, FULL MOON

I felt rotten today. It's my mother's fault for singing 'My Way' at two o'clock in the morning at the top of the stairs. Just my luck to have a mother like her. There is a chance my parents could be alcoholics. Next year I could be in a children's home.

The dog got its own back on my father. It jumped up and knocked down his model ship, then ran into the garden with the rigging tangled in its feet. My father kept saying, 'Three months' work down the drain', over and over again.

The spot on my chin is getting bigger. It's my mother's fault for not knowing about vitamins.

Saturday   January 3rd

I shall go mad through lack of sleep! My father has banned the dog from the house so it barked outside my window all night. Just my luck! My father shouted a swear-word at it. If he's not careful he will get done by the police for obscene language.

I think the spot is a boil. Just my luck to have it where everybody can see it. I pointed out to my mother that I hadn't had any vitamin C today. She said, 'go and buy an orange, then'. This is typical.

She still hasn't worn the lurex apron.

I will be glad to get back to school.

Sunday   January 4th
SECOND AFTER CHRISTMAS

My father has got the 'flu. I'm not surprised with the diet we get. My mother went out in the rain to get him a vitamin C drink, but as I told her, 'It's too late now'. It's a miracle we don't get scurvy. My mother says she can't see anything on my chin, but this is guilt because of the diet.

The dog has run off because my mother didn't close the gate. I have broken the arm on the stereo. Nobody knows yet, and with a bit of luck my father will be ill for a long time. He is the only one who uses it apart from me. No sign of the apron.

Monday   January 5th

The dog hasn't come back yet. It is peaceful without it. My mother rang the police and gave a description of the dog. She made it sound worse than it actually is: straggly hair over its eyes and all that. I really think the police have got better things to do than look for dogs, such as catching murderers. I told my mother this but she still rang them. Serve her right if she was murdered because of the dog.

My father is still lazing about in bed. He is supposed to be ill, but I noticed he is still smoking!

Nigel came round today. He has got a tan from his Christmas holiday. I think Nigel will be ill soon from the shock of the cold in England. I think Nigel's parents were wrong to take him abroad.

He hasn't got a single spot yet.

Tuesday   January 6th
EPIPHANY, NEW MOON

The dog is in trouble!

It knocked a meter-reader off his bike and messed all the cards up. So now we will all end up in court I expect. A policeman said we must keep the dog under control and asked how long it had been lame. My mother said it wasn't lame, and examined it. There was a tiny model pirate trapped in its left front paw.

The dog was pleased when my mother took the pirate out and it jumped up the policeman's tunic with its muddy paws. My mother fetched a cloth from the kitchen but it had strawberry jam on it where I had wiped the knife, so the tunic was worse than ever. The policeman went then. I'm sure he swore. I could report him for that.

I will look up 'Epiphany' in my new dictionary.

Sue Townsend, *The Secret Diary of Adrian Mole Aged 13¾*

2 Work in small groups. Using the plot details and character outlines given below, work out a story line for a bestselling thriller novel. Alternatively, you could work out a story line for a different kind of book, romance or science fiction or a novel based on the story of an ordinary young person's life.

Characters

Central character = girl of about 16. Pupil at a smart boarding school. She is the daughter of a famous rock star of the 60s and 70s.

Boyfriend = about the same age, pupil at local comprehensive; singer in a small group which is beginning to become known and has been asked to perform in various European countries.

Girl's mother = very smart, very rich. Probably rather nasty?

Girl's stepfather = international financier who is mixed up in the drug business.

Girl's father = still young, easy-going, charming. Apparently not much to him.

Plot

Set in any British city. (It should preferably be one that all of you know quite well.)

Main incident concerns kidnap attempt by gang who want a huge ransom.

Assignment 3 **Coming to conclusions ('Did you see . . . ?')**

3·1 | **Ratings**

What you need: *List of top ten TV programmes*
(optional) *for a given week. (Available from Sunday papers)*

Keep a diary of the programmes you watch during one particular week. Work in groups to prepare a report on your group's viewing habits.

1 Which were the top ten programmes? How did these compare with the ratings list for the whole country?

2 Why do you think the programmes you chose to watch were popular? Why do you think your choice differed from the ratings list? (If it did.)

3 What were the average number of hours watched? Do you think this is too much? Did the amount of time surprise you?

4 Did most people watch all of a programme or only fragments while doing something else? Which programmes made people concentrate on what they were watching?

5 Which types of programme were most popular (e.g. sports, films, music programmes)?

6 What do you remember about what you saw on television during the week?

7 Do you record TV programmes on a video recorder? Which do you keep and why?

8 Do you use television only for entertainment?

3·2 | **What makes a good programme?**
What you need: Copies of the next week's
(optional)   Radio and TV Times.

Work in groups of four people. Decide on four programmes to watch
during the next week. They should each be a different type of programme,
chosen from the list below.

TYPES OF PROGRAMME

1 Quiz show
2 Chat show
3 Comedy
4 Soap opera
5 Children's programme
6 Main news
7 Wildlife documentary
8 Current affairs documentary
9 Music programme
10 Drama serial
11 Play
12 Sports programme
13 Special interest programme

When you've chosen the four programmes, you should then select a
different person to introduce a discussion of each of them.

You could discuss some of these points:
– Was the programme too long/too short?
– Were there times when you lost interest? When and why?
– Was it interesting to look at?
– Were the characters believable?
– What did you think of the presenter?
– Was it transmitted at the right time?
– Did it have a good story?
– Would you have altered any of the items in the programme?
– Do you think it was a good programme of its type? Why?

3·3   **Presenting the news**

What you need: *A collection of ten newspaper*
headlines and brief outlines
of the various different stories.

Before you start on this exercise, watch some television news bulletins on
the various channels and notice how they are prsesented, in what order
the items are shown, what pictures are used and so on. How do the
various news programmes differ?

Work in small groups. Read the story outlines and decide which items
you would choose for a 5-minute television news bulletin. You should
take the following points into account:

1 The order you will use the items in. Which are the most important
    stories? Why? How would you justify your choices?
2 Make sure you have variety. For example, not all the stories should be
    political or human interest or just about the UK.
3 Think about how you plan to present each of the items. For example,
    you could use direct reporting, interviews with the people concerned,
    interviews with experts or film with a voice-over. Which method would
    be most suitable for each of the news items you are covering?
4 Plan the visual side of your presentation. What film could you use?
    What could be done with graphics (e.g. maps, drawings, and so on)?
5 Think of how you can get the important points across quickly.
6 Balance serious and light items.

3·4   **How television affects us**   Discuss some or all of the following topics:

1   What are the main points made by the speaker in the speech on television and education printed below? Do you think that she is right in what she says?

'We could compare the effect of television on family life to the effect of inviting a stranger to come and live in your house. Just as a stranger would occupy and interest your children, so television will involve and entertain them, leaving you more time for other activities. But the effect on family life doesn't stop there. The example set by a stranger might contradict the way you've taught your children to behave. Similarly, the scenes shown on television can contradict the moral code you've tried to teach them. We all know that television has both good and bad effects on family life. What we must remember is that this kind of influence, whether of a stranger or of television, can be difficult for parents to control.

Now I'd like to discuss the effect of television on children's education. There are many ways in which television influences children's learning. For instance, one major consequence of watching television is to improve visual skills at the expense of written ones. I am of the opinion that education must learn to cope with this change.

I want to look at two main areas of change: how children remember and how they concentrate. First, memory. Young children primarily use visual memory. And since television is a visual medium it reinforces this habit. And as in most TV programmes the picture is more important than the words, children may remember the image and forget the information. But at the moment education depends on verbal memory rather than visual. So education either has to change to use children's visual memory or it has to actively teach children other ways of remembering.

New evidence suggests that television has an effect on another learning skill: concentration. If children are bored by the programme on one channel they will switch over to another. They channel hop from one programme to another looking for the interesting bit rather than watching one programme to the end. So they are learning to expect constant stimulation. Therefore in the search for stimulation they become used to receiving a series of short unrelated extracts on different subjects. Consequently their ability to concentrate on one subject for a period of time is suffering. Once again, we shall have to actively teach children how to concentrate.

But I don't think that television is altogether bad for children's education. It produces articulate children, children with a good visual awareness, children who respond well to information presented in an interesting way. Education has to learn to adapt to the needs of such children. Teachers have to learn to beat television at its own game.'

(a) How do you think teachers can help children to remember things which aren't shown as pictures?

(b) What can be done to help children concentrate more easily?

(c) How can teachers use television to help children to learn?

(d) Is it possible to help people to look at television programmes in a different way, so that they aid learning as well as providing entertainment?

(e) What makes it obvious that this is a formal speech and not just someone talking casually? Try to pick out the various ways in which the speaker puts her arguments forward.

2 Would you stop a child of 8–10 years old from watching any of the programmes on television at the moment? If so, why?

3 What do you think are the aims of children's television? How do you think children's television differs from the rest of the programmes on offer?

Assignment 4 **Small talk**

| 4·1 |

Slang   Here's a transcript of some 16 and 17 year olds talking (in London, 1983) about the slang they use. Much of it may be out of date now, but you might find it interesting to compare their slang words with the ones you use.

'What's a wally?'
'People I don't like.'
'It's a South coast name for a pickled gherkin.'
'Do you call people wallies?'
'Yes.'

'Do you call people gherkins?'

'No. Not usually.'

'A wally's just someone who does something really stupid, like spilling their drink or something.'

'A real prannie or a prat.'

'So it's a real insult?'

'Oh, it's not as bad as calling people Brenties or grockels.'

'Why? What are Brenties?'

'Oh, they're . . . really distasteful people.'

'What do you say when something's really good?'

'Oh, you'd say it was groovy . . .'

'Or cool.'

'Or neat. And when someone's done something bad to somebody else but it's still funny you'd say that was "well wicked".'

'And "well bad". That can mean either something is really amazing or just the opposite. Like when you come out of an exam or something and you say "That was well bad". It depends on how you say it.'

'You pick stuff up from the telly, too. Saying something's "classic" or "fascist" for instance.'

'Or "bottle"?'

'No. That's untrendy now. Couple of years ago, maybe.'

'It's naff. Now you'd say someone's "cool" or a "dude".'

'What about words like "triff" or "brill"?'

'Oh, they've gone out. It's really embarrassing to use them.'

Here's another transcript of young people talking about slang. This time it was in Oldham in the 1950s. They're talking about the words men use to refer to women.

'I'd call her a bird or a bint or a wench.'
'If she was an ugly type . . . a boot, or a wench or a judy.'
'If a girl was walking on the other side of the street I might say there's a bit of stuff or a bit of crackling.'
'Oh, bits of skirt, bits of fluff, tarts, brides.'
'To her face, if I didn't know her . . . I'd call her "love" I suppose.'
'Oh, they call us birds and bits and judies . . .'
'And brides and pieces. Makes you feel common.'
'What would you like them to call you?'
'Darling.'

In 1983 not a great deal had changed. The girls still objected to the names they were called.

'Some people call me the wife. That really bugs me.'
'His bit. His bit of skirt. Really patronising.'
'The other half.'
'The better half.'

1 Work together to compile a short dictionary of slang words you use or have heard other people use. You could divide them into categories; for example, you could put all the words which mean something is good or bad together, all the slang words which refer to girls or women and so on.

2 What words do you use to talk about the opposite sex?

What does your list of words suggest about attitudes to men and women in our society? For example, what idea would the word 'princess' suggest about a woman? Would it be the same kind of idea as the word 'prince' used about a man?

Some of the girls in London and Oldham objected to the way men talked about them. Can you think of some other words which might be more acceptable?

4·2   **Polite conversation**   Work in pairs for this exercise, but don't choose your partner yourself. You could use some kind of random system for selection; for example, you could write out the letters of the alphabet twice, tear up the paper so that each letter is on a separate small piece, put all the letters into a bowl, get each person to pick one out and then make up the pairs from those holding the same letters.

One person in each pair should take the part of a pupil who has been asked to look after a stranger of your own age who is visiting your school. The other partner takes the part of the stranger. You have to talk to each other for 4 or 5 minutes while waiting for the head to return. Here are some possible topics of conversation:

1 Journey to the school.
2 First visit?
3 Reason for visit?
4 Present school.
5 Where you live.
6 Interesting points about the school.
7 Opinions of the good things about the school.
8 What subjects?
9 Interests.

It's up to both sides to keep the conversation going, although the host should start the talking.

When you've finished, change partners, using the same random system and do the same exercise, except that instead of playing the part of the new pupil one of you should pretend to be the *parent* of the prospective pupil.

What kind of questions would you ask? How would you cope with the age difference? How would you avoid being rude by asking questions which are too personal? How do you think the parent would cope with the situation?

When you've finished the role play, discuss the differences you found between the two conversations.

PERSUASION AND ARGUMENT

Assignment 1 **Personal persuasion**

'Mum ...'   This is a transcript of a conversation between a 16-year-old girl and her mother. The girl is trying to persuade her mother that she should be allowed to come home after midnight on the following Saturday night.

DEBBIE: Mum ...

MOTHER: Mmm ...

DEBBIE: You know that party I said I was going to on Saturday night ...

MOTHER: What party?

DEBBIE: You know. I told you. Susan's party.

MOTHER: Oh yes. Susan with the glasses.

DEBBIE: That's right. Well, I was thinking. You see, it's going to be one of those late parties where nobody gets there much before about 10, and if I have to be home by midnight ...

MOTHER: You know what we decided, don't you? You're still a bit too young to be out so late at night. You know what your father thinks. And besides, there are so many stories in the local papers . . . I can't sleep when you're out at night. Your sister was never allowed out as late as you are. I'm sure she'd agree with us. You ask her. And these parties, well, from what you hear it's all drugs and orgies anyway. There was a story on the telly the other day about some boys who got into some party where they weren't invited and smashed the whole place up and one of the guests was badly beaten up too. Oh, no. You're not going. I can tell you that right now.

How do you think Debbie could have persuaded her mother? How could she have prevented her mother arguing *herself* into a stubborn refusal to listen to what Debbie had to say?

Here's another possible version of their conversation:

DEBBIE: Well, I was thinking. You see, it's going to be one of those late parties where nobody gets there much before about 10. And if I've got to be home by midnight . . .

MOTHER: You know what we've always said, Debbie.

DEBBIE: Yes, of course I do. And of course you're right. It's only sensible to be careful. I mean, I know people who are allowed out till 3 o'clock in the morning, and I can see that that's not right. It's just that this Saturday is Susan's birthday and she's having a special party. There aren't even going to be that many people there – just a few friends who I know and her cousin and some of his friends. And they must be nice, they're all at college. Ever so clever, so Susan says. And her parents will be there – upstairs, watching the telly or something. So there's not much that can happen, is there?

MOTHER: Yes but . . . That's not the point. It's not that I don't trust you and your friends. We think you've got very nice friends . . . It's coming home, that's really the problem.

DEBBIE: Actually, Susan doesn't live far. It's walking distance really, you know. And of course I'd never walk it on my own.

MOTHER: What if there wasn't anyone coming this way? And supposing you were offered a lift? By someone who was drunk? You know what they say about young people and drink. There are so many accidents. Only the other day . . .

DEBBIE: Oh, I wouldn't take a lift. I'm not silly, Mum. And as for someone coming my way, I'm sure when you were younger you weren't ever short of someone to see you home, were you? I bet you weren't. I'll have to ask Dad. Anyway, there's always

Sharon. She only lives up the road, we could come back together. And she does judo.

MOTHER: Oh, Sharon's going, is she? Well, if her mother is letting her come back late . . .

DEBBIE: Oh mum, you are wonderful. I knew you'd agree. You always understand. You're not like some mothers . . . some of them are so horrible. Let me give you a kiss . . .

How did Debbie persuade her mother to let her stay out late? Can you pick out some of the points she made? What did you think of the *way* she went about persuading her?

1·2 **'You don't mind, do you?'** Work with a partner. One of you should play the part of the parent, either mother, father or other person in authority; the other should be a young person trying to persuade him or her to give permission for one of the following:

1 Going on holiday with friends.
2 Going to an open-air concert instead of on a family outing.
3 Getting more pocket money.
4 Going to an all night party.
5 Dropping a school subject.

1·3 | **'Why don't you ...?'** Work with a partner. One of you should take the part of the persuader and the other of the person who is trying to resist being persuaded. Either choose one of the following topics or select another issue that you feel strongly about. Think of as many arguments as you can and also think of the ways which would be most effective in persuading someone of your own age to come round to your point of view. For example, if you decide to choose stopping smoking as your topic, you might stress the unpleasant impression smokers make on non-smokers.

1 Vegetarianism.
2 Meat eating.
3 Animal liberation.
4 Stopping smoking/taking drugs/drinking/glue sniffing.
5 Taking up a particular sport or hobby.
6 Keeping a pet.

Here are some arguments you might use to persuade someone to stop eating meat:

1 It's unhealthy – too many animal fats. Possible heart disease later in life.
2 Vegetables provide a high fibre diet which is healthy.
3 Meat contains many extra chemicals, antibiotics, etc., which are given to animals and which we eat, not knowing what the substances are and having no control over them.
4 Animals are kept in poor and overcrowded conditions because of our demands for meat.
5 Human beings become brutalised because they support the unnecessary wholesale slaughter of animals.
6 Meat is more expensive than a vegetarian diet.
7 Eating meat is inefficient. We could use the same amount of land to produce more vegetable food for the world's starving.

Here are some arguments you might use to persuade a vegetarian that eating meat was a good idea:

1 Meat provides a supply of high-quality protein which is necessary for our health. Although supplies of protein can be obtained from non-meat foods you must eat more carefully to obtain the same results.
2 It can be bad for growing children and young people to give up meat entirely.
3 Animals are humanely slaughtered and do not suffer unnecessarily.
4 If we didn't need to keep animals for meat we would be unlikely to rear and look after them on farms. There would be far fewer animals born.
5 Animals are well looked after because farmers are interested in getting a good price for them and unhealthy animals don't make a good profit.
6 A meat diet is much less trouble than a vegetarian one.

7 It also allows for a greater variety of dishes and has a stronger taste.
8 Animals are needed to graze pasture, without them huge areas of this country would revert to wilderness and the people who had previously worked the land would be unemployed.

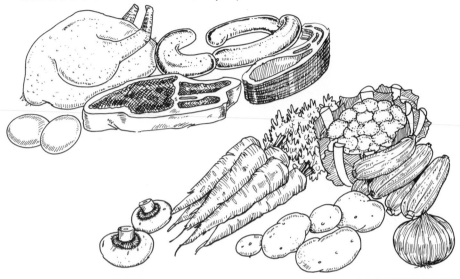

Assignment 2 **Persuasion to buy**

2·1   **Advertising**

What you need: *A collection of newspaper and magazine ads.*

1 Make a list of television, radio and poster advertisements you can remember for the various types of products listed below. Collect some examples of advertisements from magazines and newspapers.

  – washing powder
  – household products (e.g. furniture polish, paint)
  – sweets and chocolates
  – tinned foods
  – frozen meals
  – puddings
  – soft drinks
  – alcoholic drinks
  – cigarettes
  – electrical goods
  – services (e.g. phone, electricity, gas)
  – cars
  – toys
  – perfume and toiletries.

2 Each of you should choose a different *printed* advertisement to talk about. You should comment on the different techniques used, say how successful you think it is and who the advertisement was aimed at (i.e. age and social group, male or female).

3 Working in groups, with each group taking two or more of the categories listed above, discuss the techniques the advertisers use to sell their various products. For example, advertisers use humour, sex, power, nature, the idea of a perfect wife and mother and so on to persuade people to buy their particular brand of product. Also look at the use of colour, vocabulary, music and product names in the various advertisements.

4 Are there any criticisms you would make of these technqiues? For example, do you think it is unfair to suggest that someone will become more desirable if s/he buys a particular kind of perfume or aftershave?

2·2　**I'm Cruella. Buy Me!**　This is an imaginary transcript of a fur coat selling itself to a potential buyer:

'(IN A PURRING VOICE) I'm a Lady. I'm a classy lady. I shop in the most expensive shops because I am a most expensive person. Only very rich people can afford to buy me. Poor little people can't afford me at all. So they say I'm cruel – Cruella they call me in some quarters. So vulgar. Such small mean minds. They talk about little animals. They mention blood. As if there would be any blood. Blood would mean piercing the fur; spoiling it – so of course we find other methods.

Clubbing is often best. I'm not suitable for the squeamish sort of person. But then it's not the squeamish sort of person who thinks to buy me. To put it plainly, they don't have the cash. Soft, wet squeamish sort of people don't make enough money to buy me. It's only successful types who can afford the real luxuries of life. So my message is – go away little man; go away little woman – I'm only interested in you if your're rich and powerful and famous. If you are ... well, I have a little place not far from the Palace ... ring the bell twice and ask for Cruella ...'

Choose one of the items given below. Then work out a sales pitch and sell yourself, using an appropriate voice and gestures. Obviously, you don't have to use the same technique as the fur coat example uses; you might choose a much more straightforward explanation of your special features.
– a toy space-craft with hundreds of gadgets;
– a custom-built car with a modified engine;
– a luxury three-piece suite;
– a very expensive and extreme high-fashion outfit;
– a personal computer with special features;
– a shampoo made from herbs, nettles, oats, etc.;
– an exercise bicycle.

2·3   **Selling bric-a-brac**   Work in pairs or small groups. Each group should decide on some items that they think they could sell to other members of the class.
  Here are some suggestions:

– old records or tapes;
– clothes you no longer wear;
– hardly used make-up or perfume;
– posters you're bored with;
– drawings, paintings, pottery, jewellery, etc. which you've made yourself;
– spare parts for bikes and other mechanical or electrical equipment;
– bits and pieces of hi-fi/stereo equipment;
– gadgets.

When you've decided what you want to sell, bring the items in and set up a stall. Then price each of the objects, not with money but with a certain number of tokens or Monopoly money. For example, you might price a poster at 25 tokens and an old coat at 40 tokens. Each of you then takes 100 tokens for currency to buy goods.
  The aim of the exercise is for each pair or group to persuade other members of the class to 'buy' their goods with the tokens. You should think about all the advantages of your product before you start; for

example, you could point out how attractive or interesting it is; say how much you have enjoyed making or wearing or hearing it; point out how useful it could be; stress your reluctance to part with it and so on. You could also demonstrate its advantages to the buyer: 'wouldn't this be useful for when that old bike of yours comes to bits again?'; 'I think you look lovely in that colour'; 'it could really brighten up your room' and so on. You might also say that you think it is a bargain at the price, and compare it with other similar goods being offered in the shops or on other stalls.

Organise the exercise by setting up two or three stalls at a time. Those not selling act as the buyers. After a given time, swap roles so that the buyers become the stall holders. Everybody should have a chance to see all the goods on offer before the sale begins as each person is limited to spending 100 tokens only.

At the end of a given period of time you should call a halt and find out which group has ended up with the most tokens.

When you've finished, discuss what you've learnt from the exercise. You could use the questions below as a starting point:

1 Were you always honest when you were selling?
2 How did you react to being persuaded to buy things?
3 Do you think the group who had the most tokens at the end of the time deserved to 'win'. Were they the best at selling? Were their goods better than others on offer?
4 Did you enjoy selling?
5 Did you have a feeling of power over those who eventually bought your goods?
6 Did those who decided to sell things they had made themselves seem to get more satisfaction out of sales than others?

Assignment 3 **Public persuasion**

3·1 | **Rhetorical devices**   or how to make a powerful and persuasive speech.
Read the list of rhetorical devices given below. Then see if you can find
examples of some of them in the two speeches printed on pages 76–78.

1 *Rhetorical questions* – questions which have their answers built into
   them; for example, 'Isn't it a shame that a rich country like ours can't
   spare food for the starving in Africa?'
2 *Addressing people directly* – for example, 'People of Britain . . .';
   'Brothers'; 'Comrades'; 'Fellow Europeans', etc.
3 *Repetition* of a word or phrase.
4 *Antithesis* – the balancing of two contrasting ideas. For example,
   'Justice is sweet. But revenge is bitter'.
5 *Alliteration* – using the same letters at the beginning of words to
   emphasise points or make your speech sound more elegant. For
   example, 'Homes fit for heroes'; 'Workers of the world unite'.
6 *Slogans* – using one memorable carefully thought-out phrase as the
   keynote which people will remember when they go away. For
   example, 'go to work on an egg'.
7 *Comparisons* – using metaphor (e.g. 'the talks are providing a bridge
   between the management and the strikers') or simile (e.g. 'the talks are
   acting like a bridge . . .') to make your idea clearer or more vivid.

8 *Bribes or threats* – what will happen to your listeners if they do or don't do as you say. For example, 'you will get increased unemployment if . . .' or 'you'll find wonderful new prosperity if . . .'

9 *Emotive vocabulary* – words which provoke an emotional response; for example, freedom, slavery, orphan, to die for your country, triumph, agony.

10 *Working up to a high point at the end of your speech* – by speeding up or raising your voice.

11 *Summarising your message at the end* – for example with a memorable phrase or exhortation.

The first extract is from a speech by the politician Lloyd George given in 1909 on Old Age Pensions:

It is rather a shame for a rich country like ours – probably the richest country in the world, if not the richest the world has ever seen – that it should allow those who have toiled all their days to end in penury and possibly starvation. (Hear, hear.) It is rather hard that an old workman should have to find his way to the gates of the tomb, bleeding and foot-sore, through the brambles and thorns of poverty. (Cheers.) We cut a new path through it (cheers) an easier one, a pleasanter one, through fields of waving corn. We are raising money to pay for the new road (cheers), aye, and to widen it so that 200,000 paupers shall be able to join in the march. (Cheers.) There are many in the country blessed by Providence with great wealth, and if there are amongst them men who grudge out of their riches a fair contribution towards the less fortunate of their fellow-countrymen they are shabby rich men. (Cheers.) We propose to do more by means of the Budget. We are raising money to provide against the evils and the sufferings that follow from unemployment. (Cheers.) We are raising money for the purpose of assisting our great friendly societies to provide for the sick and the widows and orphans. We are providing money to enable us to develop the resources of our own land. (Cheers.) I do not believe any fair-minded man would challenge the justice and the fairness of the objects which we have in view in raising this money.

The second extract is from a speech by Martin Luther King given in 1963 on the repeal of the United States' laws discriminating between black and white citizens:

I say to you today, my friends, that in spite of the difficulties and frustrations of the moment I still have a dream. It is a dream deeply rooted in the American dream.

I have a dream that one day this nation will rise up and live out the true meaning of its creed: 'We hold these truths to be self-evident; that all men are created equal.'

I have a dream that one day on the red hills of Georgia the sons of former slaves and the sons of former slave owners will be able to sit down together at the table of brotherhood . . .

I have a dream that my four little children will one day live in a nation where they will not be judged by the colour of their skin but by the content of their character.

I have a dream today . . .

3·2   **Holding the purse-strings**   A benefactor who used to be a pupil at your school has donated a substantial sum (between £5,000 and £10,000) to your school. The terms of the gift are that school pupils are to decide how it will be spent.

Work in small groups. Each group should select a project to put forward for approval. There are some suggestions for possible projects given below, but obviously if you have another and better idea you should put that forward instead:

1 Minibus.
2 Improvement to sports facilities.
3 Scholarships for language students to exchange with foreign schools for a term.
4 Redecoration of the whole building.
5 Improvements to the canteen or dining area.
6 Resident artist, writer or musician for a year.

You should plan the arguments in favour of your proposition carefully, forestalling any objections that you think may be made.

The class should then meet to hear the various propositions put forward. One representative from each group speaks to persuade the others of the benefits of your chosen scheme.

There should then be a general discussion of the various proposals led by a chairperson and finally a vote on which proposal to put forward. Obviously, each person should try to have an open mind for this final discussion and vote on the scheme which seems to be the most advantageous for the school.

3·3 **School food – canvassing opinion** Read the article printed below about one school's campaign to change its pupils' eating habits.

Fat of the land

DENNIS CARTER

All interested in the future health of the nation should thank Nottinghamshire's education catering officer, Anne Carter (*TES*, November 22) for her attempts to change the high-fat, high-sugar diets of children towards fresh fruit and vegetables and high fibre. As head of a school which has been campaigning on this issue for 18 months now, it was most heartening to read of the various steps being taken by Nottinghamshire and Sheffield.

Unfortunately, however, this is still very much a minority response to the growing mountain of evidence linking fats and sugars to the high incidence of heart disease. The more common response is that of the Stockport parents: "let 'em eat what they like".

With the nationwide dominance of the cafeteria system this decade such attitudes have led to appallingly dangerous dietary possibilities for our children. Stories are legion of the daily molehill of chips and the pocketing of dinner money change for the purchase of sweets after school. So few controls exist in most cafeterias that this slow poisoning of future generations is easy to achieve.

The attitude of "if they want chips let them have chips", though, represents an absolute abrogation of our generation's responsibility for the health of the nation. As adults we all have responsibilities towards children; this surely is one of the things a sense of community should involve.

In our school it was the *World in Action* films early in 1984 which acted as catalysts for action. We had avoided a cafeteria system, helped by the lack of a central dining area. There were, therefore, controls built into our dispersed system of dining. Our campaign was launched in the usual ways with visits from dieticians and wholefood suppliers. Parents as well as children were involved and the only resistance came from a tiny minority who thought that multiplication tables and spelling lists were our business, not diet.

The first target for attack was the chip, which became the scallop (less fried surface area) and this was served only once a week. The jacket potato and the part-wholemeal bread roll, meanwhile, were being introduced and became popular, but never in direct competition with their fried cousins. More salads were made available and I discovered that take up increased dramatically if I spoke up in favour of salad eating.

Once we had introduced these changes we let them run and no major new initiative in the school meal has been taken since. I feel that the next campaign needs to be waged against food additives but realize the difficulties due to buying contracts already entered into by the local authority.

Our next major success was in our wholefoods tuckshop run by parents every morning. Previously we had never had a tuckshop so we were able to launch ours as a completely new venture. Suppliers of wholefood snacks were not difficult to find and these snacks have become just as popular as crisps and jammy dodgers. At present we sell nuts, sultanas (very popular), raisins, crunchy bars and wholewheat crisps (a sell-out every time).

These days I smile with irony when I glance at the litter outside the school front door and see *Jordan's Original Crunchy* wrappers dancing cheek to cheek in the wind with *Allinson's Wholewheat Crisps* bags. I console myself with the thought that perhaps, in a school based on real first-hand experiences, such litter, although a nuisance, is a most effective way of consolidating those healthy foods in the minds of the children.

Dennis Carter is head of Taliesin junior school, Shotton, Deeside, Clwyd.

Working in small groups, devise a questionnaire to find out opinions about possible changes to the food available in your school. Your questionnaire should be suitable for as wide a variety of people as possible, including pupils, parents, teaching and catering staff. Make sure your questions are simple to answer. For example, you could use some of the following techniques:

1 *Put in order of preference the following main dishes.* (You should give up to five examples.)
2 *Tick one of the alternatives from this list:* How often do you bring a packed lunch? Always? More than once a week? Once a week? Never?
3 *Choose two alternatives from this list:* The best way to improve school meals would be by: . . . .(Give a list of six or more ideas.)

3·4 **The early school day – gathering evidence** It has been suggested that this country should change the times of the school day so that it runs from 8.45 in the morning to 2.00 in the afternoon. This system is used successfully in other countries.

Your aim is to gather evidence for a debate to be held at your school on this subject. You need to find out the opinions and ideas of as many different people as possible – particularly those who are connected with the school. For example, pupils, parents and teaching and non-teaching staff.

Each group should work out a questionnaire suitable for all these different groups of people. You can, of course, include questions which would only be appropriate, say, for the pupils to answer.

Here is an example of a question which could be given to pupils only and which could provide useful evidence for argument on the subject:

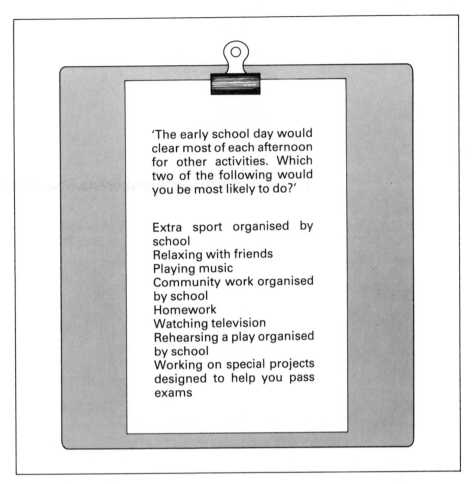

'The early school day would clear most of each afternoon for other activities. Which two of the following would you be most likely to do?'

Extra sport organised by school
Relaxing with friends
Playing music
Community work organised by school
Homework
Watching television
Rehearsing a play organised by school
Working on special projects designed to help you pass exams

1 You need to think of questions which will allow people to express opinions in a simple yes/no answer.
2 You need to work out in advance what views staff, pupils and parents might be expected to hold so that you can produce the right sort of questions.

When you have designed your questionnaire, which should have between ten and twenty questions on it, go out and ask as many different people as possible to fill it in. Then each of your groups should report the results to the rest of the class. When you make your report, don't just give a list of figures; try to draw general conclusions from the information you've obtained. For example, if you asked the sample question given above, you might conclude from the answers you were given that most pupils would spend their time listening to music and talking to friends. However, a substantial minority would choose to do extra work for their exams.

When each group has finished giving its results, you should work out together what useful evidence you have collected for the debate and think about how it could be used.

3·5   **Age and the law – using anecdotes in argument**   Work in small groups. Look at the list below which gives the ages at which young people can gain certain rights by law:

From birth

You can have an account in your name with a bank or a building society
You can have premium bonds in your name
You can have a passport of your own (if one of your parents signs the application form)

At age 5

You can drink alcohol legally in private

At age 7

You can draw money from a post office or savings account

At age 10

You can be convicted of a criminal offence if it is proved that you knew the difference between right and wrong

At age 12

You can buy a pet animal

At age 13

You can be employed for a certain number of hours a week

At age 14

You can be held fully responsible for a crime
You can be fingerprinted if you are in custody and charged
You can be convicted of a sexual offence (applies to boys only)
You can pawn an article in a pawn shop
You can go into a pub, but not drink or buy alcohol there

At age 15

You can be sent to Borstal
You can be sent to prison to await trial (applies to boys only)

At age 16

You can buy premium bonds
You can sell scrap metal
You can buy cigarettes or tobacco
You can join a trade union
You can leave school
You can choose your own doctor
You can claim social security benefit

You can work full-time
You can have sexual intercourse (applies to girls only: if a girl under sixteen has sexual intercourse, her partner, the boy, is liable to prosecution)
You can leave home with your parents' consent
You can get married with one parent's consent
You can drink wine or beer with a meal in a restaurant

You can buy fireworks
You can hold a licence to drive a moped, motor cycle, certain tractors or invalid carriages

At age 17

You can hold a licence to drive any vehicle except certain heavy ones
You can be sent to prison
You can appear before adult courts
You can engage in street trading

At age 18

You can leave home without your parents' consent
You can get married without your parents' consent
You can vote
You can act as executor of a person's will
You can make a will
You can bet
You can change your name
You can apply for a passport
You can buy and sell goods
You can own houses and land
You can buy on hire purchase
You can apply for a mortgage
You can sue and be sued
You can go abroad to sing, play or perform professionally
You can sit on a jury
You can be a blood donor
You can buy alcohol
You can drink alcohol in a pub

At age 21

You can stand in a Parliamentary or local election
You can drive any mechanically propelled vehicle
You can hold a licence to sell alcohol
You can take part in a homosexual relationship (applies to boys only)
You can adopt a child

You should choose one or more of the items from the list on page 82 and work out an argument to persuade people that it should either stay the same or be changed. For example, you might choose to argue a case for raising the school leaving age from 16 to 18. In that case, you should make a list of points in favour of your argument. What you should also do is to think of some examples from your own experience to illustrate the strength of your argument. Here's an example:

I think the school leaving age should be raised to 18. My brother left school as soon as he could after his sixteenth birthday. On his first day out of school he just stayed in bed all day and refused to go out even though my parents tried everything to make him stay at school. He said he just wanted to go out to work. The trouble was that he didn't have any exams and the school wouldn't give him much of a reference. So the only job he could get was working in a green-grocer's part time. And he was lucky to get that. He's still there and he's got no prospects. He says now that he would have stayed on at school if he'd had to and he thinks he might have got some exams, or at least done some more woodwork which he was quite good at. The point is that there are a lot of people like my brother. When they're sixteen, all they want to do is get out of school at fast as they can. If they had to stay on by law they might *have* to learn some sort of skill or something just to fill in the time. And the school could organise work experience so that they could get some sort of idea of what it was like out at work. My brother said he didn't have the faintest idea what it would be like in a job. Of course, they'd have to work out how people were going to use their extra time at school pretty carefully or it would be a terrible waste . . .

If you were arguing the opposite point, that the school leaving age should be left as it is at the moment, you might include an anecdote about someone you know in a family of five children where the parents just can't afford to keep another child at school for an extra 2 years. He or she would have to work in all his or her spare time for terrible wages at whatever job s/he could get. This would lead to greater unemployment because employers would use school pupils as cheap part-time labour instead of employing people full time at a proper wage.

Assignment 4 **Argument and debate**

| 4·1 |

Hat debate   A hat debate works like this: a number of topics are written out and then divided up so that each topic is on a separate piece of paper. Each person then draws one of the topics out of a hat and has to prepare notes for a short speech supporting the subject s/he has picked. It doesn't matter that in fact you may believe the complete opposite of the position you have to argue or even have no particular interest in the subject. You should still find at least two or three arguments in support of the topic you have chosen.

LIST OF POSSIBLE TOPICS

1 Team games at school should be voluntary.
2 The Queen should abdicate so that we have a younger monarch.
3 Top sports players are massively overpaid.
4 New Year and Birthday Honours – kinghthoods, OBEs, etc. – are a useful incentive.
5 English spelling is totally illogical and should be reformed.
6 It's wrong to judge people by the way they talk.
7 It's unfair to judge people by their exam results.
8 Smoking should be totally banned in public places.
9 Penalties for serious driving offences are not heavy enough.
10 Religious schools should be abolished.
11 Public schools should be abolished.
12 Sunday trading is bad for family life.
13 The Church should allow women to become priests.
14 Breakfast TV is a dreadful waste of money.
15 All school leavers should have a basic political education.
16 We should never give in to threats from terrorists.
17 Free will is an illusion.
18 We should have low flat rate fares on public transport to discourage private cars.
19 Schools should not restrict pupils' hairstyles or make-up.
20 The popular press is nothing more than a series of telly articles and adulation of stars and royalty.
21 Experimentation on human embryos sets a dangerous precedent in tampering with human life.
22 'Nature' has more influence on our personalities than 'nurture'.
23 The arts should not be subsidised with public money.
24 Every woman should have the right to an abortion if she wishes one.

4·2   **Balloon debate**   The idea of a balloon debate is to decide which of six selected characters is most worth saving from extinction.
It works like this:

1 Choose six characters. These should include some or all of the following:

Real and fictional characters
Males and females
People from the past or present
Different kinds of occupations
Famous people
Different nationalities
Well-known characters from your school or area

As an example, a recent balloon went up containing:

Queen Elizabeth I
Pythagoras
A character from a TV soap opera
A Labour MP
A popular musician
The Prime Minister of Jamaica

Another balloon contained:

Jane Austen, the novelist
Pontius Pilate
The Princess of Wales
The Prime Minister
A senior judge
A famous woman athlete

Obviously, you should choose people who interest you or who have recently been in the news. It's usually a good idea to make the list as varied as possible.

2 The story is that these six people are in a hot-air balloon. If any of them is to survive, four of the balloonists must be thrown out immediately. When that has been decided, one of the others must also go, leaving one lone survivor. The decisions about who is to be sacrificed are made by the spectators, who base their decisions on the quality of the balloonists' arguments.

3 Decide who is going to represent each character. The rest of the class are the spectators who decide which characters will be thrown out.

4 The balloonists should draw lots to decide which order they are to speak in. Each character is to speak for only 3 or 4 minutes. The speech should contain:
   (a) A brief biographical background.
   (b) The main features of the character's life and achievements.
   (c) The reasons why he or she should remain in the balloon.
   (d) The reasons why others should be thrown out first.

   (*The Dictionary of National Biography, Who's Who* and newspaper and magazine articles should give some useful information.)

5 When the balloonists have made their speeches, the spectators should then comment on the merits of the candidates. If a spectator feels strongly that a particular candidate should remain then it is a good idea to restate his or her strong points so that other spectators can be influenced further before they vote.

6 All spectators should now make their first-round votes for two survivors.

7 When the votes have been counted, the two survivors should speak again, answering points made by spectators and showing what they can offer to the world which their companion can't.

8 The spectators now vote to choose the one survivor.

4·3   **Formal debate (1)**   You can have a debate on almost any topic which has two or more possible points of view. The rules for a formal debate are printed in Appendix II on page 123. Read the arguments made in the sample debate on fashion. You could then hold your own debate on the same subject, using some of the arguments given in the sample and adding others of your own. (For advice to speakers in a debate, see page 91.)

Sample debate

'This house believes that fashion is just a commercial racket.'

Proposition (for)

SPEAKER ONE
Introduction – my arguments will prove that fashion is no more than a commercial racket designed to make money at the consumer's expense.
1 Fashion exploits people's wish to look up-to-date.
2 In order to be accepted and admired by friends you have to follow fashion. Ask youself how you choose your clothes.
3 So perfectly serviceable clothes are no longer 'wearable'. Society jeers at those who wear last season's colours, shapes, etc.
4 Fashion is manipulated by big business so that clothes change each season. Look at the enormous number of fashion magazines, the news made by Paris fashion shows, the window displays in all the stores. TV and film stars, musicians and celebrities have their clothes analysed and commented on. Many stars even endorse design ranges themselves. Think about the ridiculous business of wearing 'designer' labels on perfectly ordinary clothes, just to show people that you're in fashion.

5 Fashion encourages poor workmanship because articles don't have to last. For example, 'fashion boots' are boots which aren't waterproof and don't stand up to much walking. You soon have to buy a new pair. This is a commercial racket.

6 It's especially young people who are encouraged to be in fashion by advertisements, etc. And it's young people who are often gullible and can't really afford the changes which fashion demands.

7 Finally, to answer what will probably be the opposition's main argument – that fashion encourages individuality. This isn't true. Fashion encourages the herd instinct. People wear fashionable clothes even if the colours and shapes are seriously unflattering. (Give example.)

8 Stand up for your individuality against the forces of fashion and support the motion.

Opposition (against)

SPEAKER TWO

Introduction – the proposer is as involved in fashion as anyone else. (Quick comment on some fashion aspect of proposer's clothing.) My argument is based on the social benefits of fashion.

1 Fashion is on the side of individuality. Think of the opposite – e.g. uniform for schools or armies. This aims to get everybody to work together and conform. Fashion is a way of stating who you are.

2 Fashion is fun. Much of the rest of of life is routine. How boring if we all dressed the same, wore our hair the same, carried identical bags. Should we all dress like the Queen or the Prime Minister or Prince Charles? There's real pleasure to be gained from dressing up and looking different.

3 Fashion is more than just saying 'this is me'. It also shows which group you belong to. Give example.

4 Changes in fashion are not part of a commercial plot. Most fashion starts with young people on the street and moves from there into the chain stores. Many fashion 'followers' buy their clothes from jumble sales or adapt them from bits and pieces which they've carefully collected. It's a very creative business.

5 Changes in fashion make comments about the mood of the country. For example, punk with its emphasis on accessories like safety pins and with dresses made out of bin liners, was commenting on young people's desire to dissent from cosy complacency. Slogan T shirts show that fashion and social conscience can go together.

6 We would be in trouble both socially and financially without fashion. My seconder will deal in more detail with the financial aspect.

7 Finally, I say that fashion is not an excuse for the exploitation of the young. It's a creative method of self expression.

Seconder – proposition (for)

SPEAKER THREE

Introduction – The Opposer has shown him/herself to be the victim of clever manipulators. S/he has believed the business propaganda.

1 Fashion doesn't show 'who your are'; it shows how much you can afford to spend on clothes. Look at mothers with young children – often not at all fashionably dressed – they have other priorities. What do their clothes say about them?

2 The fashion con-men, not just clothes designers and manufacturers, but all the media as well, encourage us to judge people by appearance rather than as real personalities. Both here and in the US there are dress consultants you can hire who will tell you how to 'dress for success'. This is the product of a sick and materialistic society – not, as the opposer asserts, a healthy sign of creativity.

3 The corruption of the fashion racket goes further than that of a mere individual. It encourages us in the West to buy, relatively cheaply, fashion items made in the sweated workshops in the East – Taiwan, Hong Kong, etc. We are fashionable only at the expense of people working long hours on very low pay.

4 We wear furs from helpless seals clubbed to death for our sakes. We use cosmetics developed through research on helpless animals. Our sensibilities are blunted by the commercial demands of the fashion industry.

5 In conclusion, fashion panders to our worst instincts: exploitation of both people and animals; superficiality in judging others; vanity in lavishing time and attention on our appearance rather than turning our talents to more important issues. Support the motion and vote for the proposition.

Seconder – Opposition (against)

SPEAKER FOUR

Introduction – I'm glad the Proposer has raised the moral level of the debate so high. But s/he has of course been drawing totally wrong conclusions, both economically and morally.

1 First, the economics. The fashion industry in this country is extremely useful to the whole economy. Since the Industrial Revolution, and before, Britain has been an important textile manufacturer. Now the British clothing industry employs large numbers of people in this country. (Examples.) We need successful industries to provide much needed jobs. Without fashion the demand for clothes and accessories would plummet.

2 The Proposer scoffed at film stars and Royalty, but actually, the Princess of Wales has done wonders for the revival of the British clothing industry. So the claims that all the money is going to the Far East are in fact misguided.

3 The proposers have tried to prove that fashion is foisted on us by a conspiracy of media people and big business. This is absolute rubbish. There has been fashion all through the ages – from long before industrialisation or the mass media. Examples: Cleopatra, cave men, etc. It is not a racket; it's an instinct. It's the wish to look our best, to show ourselves to be part of a particular group. We don't necessarily want to look like a page from *Vogue* or *The Face*; we just want to enjoy being 'in fashion'.

Some advice for speakers in a debate

1 Four main speakers: prepare speeches in advance – make notes of your main points on postcards. *Don't* write out your whole speech word for word.

2 Plan to start your speech in a lively and interesting way. For example, with an anecdote, newspaper quotation, appropriate joke, etc. Also end your speech emphatically, don't just dry up and sit down.

3 Use evidence to support your ideas,
   e.g. personal experiences
       experiences of friends, family, etc.
       information from news media
       statistics – from news media/*Social Trends* (published
              annually by the government)/opinion polls/
              election results, etc.
       case histories, examples of incidents, etc.

4 Use rhetorical devices (see pp. 75–76) and include humour where appropriate.

5 Think about how you stand to address the House. Don't talk to the ceiling or to your shoes. Use eye contact to convince the House and the opposing team of speakers.

6 Consider how you speak. Are you guilty of any of the following?
    Mumbling
    Gabbling
    Swallowing the ends of your sentences
    Droning on on one tone
    Um-ing and er-ing
    Pausing for ages between sentences
    Giggling
    Repeating the same idea over and over again
    Saying 'sort of'; 'you know'; 'I mean'; 'really'; 'like'.

7 Try to answer the arguments of the other side with convincing arguments of your own.

4·4   **Formal debate (2)**   Hold a debate on one of the topics given below and overleaf or on one of the Hat debate topics listed on page 84 or on a subject that is topical at the moment. All topics should be prefaced with the words *'This house . . .'*

1 Believes that Trades Unions have outlived their usefulness.
2 Would abolish private schools.
3 Believes that religion has done more harm than good.

4 Believes that Britain needs its own nuclear weapons.
5 Has confidence in Her Majesty's government.
6 Can see no point in getting married.
7 Would raise the school leaving age to 18.
8 Believes space exploration to be a waste of resources.
9 Believes that positive discrimination is the best way to achieve equal opportunities for minority groups.
10 Believes that Britain has become too much like the 51st state of the USA.
11 Believes that femininity is more persuasive than feminism.
12 Believes that there is no such thing as a just war.

PART II

Points of View

ROOTS AND ORIGINS

| 1 | **Dialect and accent** |

DOMINO

Mi enta de club, it waz quiet;
Mi start fe mek me way up de stears
Mi ear noize
Ellis, Brown, Porter an Findley play domino.

Ellis atel Findley fi rub it up
Findley atel im fe shut up;
Brown atel Findley fe play
Porter noh sae noting.

Brown warn look cool,
So im tun up im jacket collar:
Ellis tink im dread
Findley look dead
Porter shave im 'ed
Im tun barl ed.

Dem clap dun de domino
Ana mek up noize.
Dem arsk one anader if dem play yet,
Iz pass dem pass

Dema run up dem mout'
Ana shout
Six up six up
One a dem shout

De game dun now.
Soh Ellis dread, Brown cool,
Findley dead an' Porter barl'ed –
Dem arl garn 'ome, garn 'ome to bed.

Rose Porter (15)

(a) How much of that poem did you understand? Can you think of any words or phrases used in your area which might not be understood in another part of the country?

(b) Look back at the section on slang on pages 63–65. Various different slangs are spoken by young people. Slang is one example of a kind of English; the poem printed above is another example; in some rural areas people use special dialect words and some families use a mixture of two languages to talk to each other. How many different kinds of English are used by the people in your class?

(c) What effect do you think having a strong accent can have? Is it a help or a handicap? Or neither? Can you think of occasions when having a strong accent would be a definite handicap? Are you at all prejudiced about particular accents?

(d) Do you think exams in spoken English should expect all children to speak more or less standard English?

2   Customs, festivals and celebrations

Christmas comes but once a year. But with Christianity no longer the dominant religion in many inner city schools, the festive season may last the whole term, be postponed until the next year or cancelled altogether as schools find different ways of coping with this major Christian festival in an increasingly multifaith society.

Peterborough's multicultural policy document, *The Way Ahead*, prepared by two local primary schools, sets out practical guidelines for a curriculum which gives 'equal validity to the variety of racial, ethnic, cultural and religious groups'. At one time the cathedral carol service was a compulsory part of Christmas. Now, for predominantly Asian schools like The Beeches, a carol service would be inappropriate for most of the pupils. The keynote is choice. Parents will be asked whether they wish their children to sing carols.

'We make no assumptions about religious beliefs,' says John Shearman, The Beeches' head. At his school Christmas this year will be 'just an assembly' with the Christmas theme treated factually from the point of view of Christian doctrine. There will be no carol service. Instead, the concert will be postponed until the end of the Spring term when there will be no pressure to sing explicitly Christian songs.

Not that it has been a bleak midwinter at The Beeches. There have been numerous celebrations this term, the biggest being Navaratri, the Hindu Festival of Nine Nights which marks the part of the Ramayana where Lord Rama defeats the 10-headed monster, Ravana. Each class made an effigy or mask of Ravana and there was a competition for the fiercest.

In early December the children celebrated Diwali, Guru Nanaks birthday, and Hannukah, the Jewish Festival of Light. Because events, assemblies and related classwork are going on throughout the term there is no need to disrupt normal activities for rehearsals for the Christmas play or carol service.

Next term's festivities include Mother's Day and St Patrick's Day. It doesn't matter if there are few or no representatives of a particular faith in the school. 'What is important is religious tolerance,' says Diana Green, head of Gladstone Primary,

and leader, with John Shearman, of the working party on *The Way Ahead*.

On the other side of the railway line is West Town school with a 30 per cent ethnic minority and a greater racial mix than The Beeches or Gladstone. Head Martin Creasey and his staff felt they wanted a Christmas celebration that kept the religious significance of the festival without offending pupils of other faiths. The theme of giving presents was chosen, and, with a little planning and ingenuity, the top junior classes wrote poems on the subject.

Their ideas ranged from giving a cake to new neighbours, taking a gift to hospital and buying a wedding present for 'Dad's friend who is marrying Jean'. Shazia thought of Diwali and someone else of his new train set. Meera read the passage from the Koran which refers to the angel appearing to Mary to announce that it is Allah's will that she should bear a son.

It is commonly recognized that Asian religions on the whole take the spiritual side of their festivals more seriously than Christians do. On the other hand most Muslim children in West Town seemed to be expecting to enjoy the trappings of Christmas along with their classmates. They said they would be celebrating with a special meal, visiting friends and relations or watching the video. 'Eid is better than Christmas', said one boy. 'For one thing there are more Eids, and you get money.'

The lower school's contribution to the Christmas entertainment will be a tableau about European customs, particularly appropriate in West Town which has children from the Italian-speaking community. Clare, who is Polish, told me she would be going to midnight mass and that there would be a special Christmas Eve supper. Although there is a Christmas tree in the corridor the decorations have been kept deliberately unChristmassy this year, said class teacher Marion Evans. Mathematical shapes and a frieze of Rangoli patterns to decorate the stage are the order of the day.

It has been left to the infant classes to provide the traditional nativity. A Sikh child has been chosen as Mary, and her father is deeply honoured. One group has just finished a Rama and Sita drama so that will almost certainly be worked into the Christ-

mas story.

It's difficult to avoid carols at Christmas, but it is possible to choose secular ones such as *Girls and boys leave your toys* and *The little drummer boy*.

'At our school,' the headmistress of a primary school in the King's Cross area of London told me, 'we choose the ones that tell the Christmas story'.

With its 70 per cent Muslim intake the emphasis is on 'the similarities rather than the differences between religions'. Here the children say that Christmas is just like Eid and their counterparts in Canon Barnet school in Hackney, will be enjoying jelly, ice cream and presents in school at Christmas.

Both these London schools are very much part of the community where teachers learn from parents and children. Communities have played an important part in the ILEA's Christmas concert which this year adopts a more positively multicultural approach than in previous years. Entitled 'London Celebrating', it draws together 400 children on stage at the Royal Festival Hall in a display of music, mime and dance. There are sixteen items with hardly a traditional carol among them.

Some schools have contributed episodes reflecting the customs of their communities. There is everything from classical Indian dance and a song about Christmas shopping with tabla and harmonium accompaniment to a nimble display of Irish dancing from members of Christ the King School, north London.

'Playing down Christmas,' to use the words of many teachers, is all very well in an inner city school with a multiracial population. But move outside Peterborough, for example, into Lincolnshire and you will hear a different story. One head feels strongly that Christianity gets a raw deal these days. 'It's not that we are racist, but after all, Britain is a Christian country.'

He says it is difficult to find up-to-date materials on the Christian faith, and believes that schools have a responsibility towards children baptized as Christians who receive no form of religious instruction at home. His school will be having a traditional carol service this year.

(a) How many different customs, festivals and celebrations are practised by members of your class and their families? Arrange to explain each of the examples you find to the class.

(b) How valuable do you think it is to maintain these customs and ceremonies? How much do you think schools should be involved?

3 | Marrying out

A question of marrying and be damned

A bride in Asian culture becomes an integral part of her husband's extended family, living with them, cooking for them and – if she works – contributing her wages to the whole family. Her behaviour, the way she dresses and even her choice of career, can all affect the pride of the family in the eyes of the community and thus transgression of the accepted rules of behaviour on the part of a daughter or potential daughter-in-law can lead to the whole family being rejected or treated with contempt.

What happens to the increasing number of young Asians who reject arranged marriages altogether and, worse still in the eyes of their parents, choose partners who are non-Asian?

Satvinder, a 25-year-old Sikh girl, knowingly courted ostracism by rejecting an arranged marriage and by choosing a Jamaican partner. She lives in West London with her boyfriend Marvin and their six-month-old daughter and has not had any contact with her family since she told them nearly a year ago of her long-standing relationship with Marvin.

Marvin had been a close friend of her brother and was popular with the family until he was revealed as a potential son-in-law. When Satvinder made her admission, her father said she was 'dead for the family', and soon after he sent her a solicitor's letter which forbade her to use the family name.

'In Sikh culture, a woman takes on the identity of her husband,' says Satvinder, 'so now I am regarded as Jamaican.'

Satvinder feels that her degree-level education caused her to question arranged marriages and – despite her family's traditional attitudes – she always felt that they understood her feelings. She was therefore surprised to find that she had been wrong:

'I came home one day and my sisters were all dressed up, and everyone looked happy, so I thought some friends were visiting. My sister came upstairs and said there was a boy downstairs who had come to see me. I didn't believe her and refused to go down.

'My sister lectured me on being a spinster, and the man who was arranging the marriage came up and told me that Western influence would cause a rootless life for me and that I would thank him in years to come. He said he was going downstairs to announce the engagement but I refused to move and eventually they all went away. I was shaking and angry and in a daze for several days. I thought it would never happen to me.'

Despite her anger, Satvinder cannot wholly reject the idea of arranged marriages and this applies to many young Asians. They resent the stereotyped and often inaccurate view that some non-Asians have, of an oppressed girl forced to share the bed of a total stranger, or locked in her room away from the temptations of the outside world. Many marriages are now semi-arranged and the boy and girl are allowed several meetings and one or two refusals. The attitudes of even traditional parents are changing gradually, as more and more young Asians are influenced by their lives in Britain.

However, even parents who think of themselves as liberal and westernised can still be shocked by their children's choice of partner. This happened to Jasvinder, a 31-year-old lecturer who came to Britain from the Punjab at the age of four:

When Jasvinder told her father of her intention to marry an Englishman, John, she says the shock was 'all over his face.'

'My parents were in shock for two days,' she says. 'They couldn't speak – not didn't want to – they just physically couldn't get the words out. My grandmother in India took to her bed for three days when she heard the news.'

Jasvinder thinks that her Father reacted in this way because he was worried about her safety in a white community: 'He thought I might be abused in some way, by a husband who drank or went off with other women.'

John and their five-year-old son are now well-loved members of the family and Jasvinder thinks that she should perhaps have introduced her boyfried more gradually into the family. 'I was afraid to mention the relationship until it was serious,' she says, 'because I knew that I would be expected to marry any boy that I brought home.'

Satvinder says that in cases where English or non-Asian girls marry Indian boys, the adaptation process is relatively painless. 'You'd be surprised how much English girls are prepared to adapt to fit in with the wishes of the family,' she says.

Neither she nor Jasvinder want to lose their Asian identity, and all the women in such mixed marriages make an effort to teach the language and culture of their background to their children. Satvinder is sad that her parents have never seen their first grandchild, but does not blame them for rejecting her: 'My parents always told me they wouldn't want to know me if I married a non-Sikh. I respect them for that. I was clear that going my own way meant rejection. My father was scared of me losing my identity, but what he could not understand is that now I am more Indian – an extra Indian – because if you marry someone of a different background you will try even harder to retain your identity and pass it on to your children.'

(a) Think of arguments in favour of arranged marriages.
(b) What problems do you think can arise in mixed marriages – marriages between members of different religions or cultures?
(c) How far do you think parents are justified in interfering with their children's marriage plans?

4 | First impressions of England

Sabir is a Ugandan Asian whose family was expelled, along with all Asians, from Uganda by President Idi Amin in August 1972. As British passport holders, his family – parents, brother and five sisters, including a baby – fled to Britain. Sabir wrote this account in 1979.

I woke up to the roaring sound of engines; my ears were deafened. I was feeling sick and felt like vomiting, but trying hard as I did, I just couldn't vomit. It was odd. It was still very dark outside. Out of the window, in the far distance below, I could see the lights of the cities of Europe. Large cities they were, but they seemed so close to each other! I gazed at them, at every group of lights that passed under me. It was beautiful and exciting. But my heart was set on England – or what I later found out – the legend of England.

Time passed rapidly; I failed to notice that these split seconds had brought us to our destination. A familiar sound brought me back into reality –

'Attention please. This is your Captain speaking. There is a slight change of plan. There is dense fog over London, so we are changing route to Stansted Airport.'

I wasn't quite sure what the announcement said; there was still the dead-buzzing inside my ears and I couldn't care less. Again the voice came through the microphone: 'We are now approaching Stansted Airport. Fasten your seat belts, please.' I felt sick and was glad when the Boeing 707 touched down.

It was 26th October, the day was dull, misty and wet, although it was not raining. I remembered the misty patch and the cool running waters on the way to my previous school. I missed it. I missed my friends, my teachers, my school and my home. I really missed everything I had left behind. I only hoped England would make up for it all.

'What time is it?' I asked my sister.

'Five past ten.'

'Look again.'

'Six past ten. Don't ask me to look again,' she muttered slowly. She was looking very tired.

'More like the break of dawn, isn't it?'

'I suppose so.'

I gave in. It was no use making conversation with her. Very unusual.

What I didn't realise then was that I was going to talk more and more about the weather through the next several years. There was nothing else to talk about, and if there was, I didn't know where to start.

Sabir's family is met by his older brothers, Sultan and Pyarali, and driven to the small terraced house in South London where they live.

As we drove through the streets, I again felt strangely curious. Was this really England? I can see these groups of Europeans but . . . the streets, they are not as broad as I had heard! The houses were not posh skyscrapers. Am I dreaming all this or am I really in England, at last? The houses were made of red brick. I gave in; but then, I saw something that really made me wonder. An old lady was walking along the footpath and she was carrying a spaniel. The thing that caught my eye was that the white spaniel was wearing something red on its back, something like a coat with no sleeves. I pointed at the spaniel. 'Look, Saida . . .' I couldn't help or stop laughing. She started laughing too. Sultan turned round from the front seat. We were at the traffic lights so that he could see exactly where I was pointing. He realised the joke and started laughing too.

'Next we'll see a cat in a blouse and skirt,' I said aloud.

The view around me was monotonous, all the buildings were made of red brick (I wondered why people didn't bother to decorate them with different coloured paints like in Uganda).

At about two, we arrived in Balham. I did not realise our journey had come to an end and I was very glad when I was informed so.

The house was numbered 76. I found it very strange at first, but I was impressed. Again it was made of bare red brick. However, much to my delight, it was fully decorated inside – nice carpet, beautiful wallpapers. It was a double-storey building, but the rooms were few compared to the size of our family. There were only three bedrooms and one 'box' room. Sultan slept in the latter. Pyarali and Pearl slept in the bedroom upstairs so that there were only two bedrooms between the nine of us. Mum and Dad and my baby sister Azima slept in one of the two rooms in the basement. Up to now, the only major problem had been to get out of Uganda. Now it seemed that there was more to it than that. The only solution was that six of us were to sleep in one bedroom. Quite a problem, wasn't it?

Imagine that you have been transported to a strange part of this country or a very different part of the world. Give an account of the differences you

notice and of what you miss about your home. You don't need any
information for this exercise, just your idea of what a particular place
might be like.

5 | **Research project: your own roots and origins**
Find out about your own roots and origins. Talk to older members of your
family about where they lived when they were young, what work they did
and how they met the person they married. How much can you find out
about your family tree?

Alternatively, you could choose to interview an older person you know
about his or her roots and origins.

MEN AND WOMEN

1 | **Equal opportunity at school**

(a) Do you think campaigns to stop sex stereotyping in school subjects are having any effect? What happens in your school?

(b) When you had to choose subjects at 14+, what influenced your choice? If your class includes both sexes, conduct a mini survey to see which subjects are taken by boys and which by girls. What are the differences?

(c) Do you think your choice of subjects would have been different in a single-sex/mixed school?

2 **Sex and politics**

WOMEN IN THE HOUSE OF COMMONS

Some facts and figures

In 1918 – the year women (over 30) got the vote, 17 women stood for election as MPs, and one woman was elected.

In 1929 – the year after women were allowed to vote at 21, 69 women stood, and 14 were elected.

In 1964 – 90 women stood, and 29 were elected. 95.4% of MPs were male and 4.6% female. This is the highest number of women in any House of Commons so far.

THE **300 GROUP**

In 1974 – 161 women stood, and 27 were elected.

In 1983 – 276 stood, and 23 were elected.

There have been eight women Cabinet ministers – ever.

Slightly over half of the electorate are women.

In 1980 the 300 group was launched to try and get 300 female MPs elected regardless of the party they represented.

Why do you think there is such an imbalance between male and female MPs?

Here are some reasons which have been put forward.

(a) Local political parties don't select women as election candidates because they don't want to take what they think of as risks; hence middle-aged, middle-class white men are the norm.

(b) Women are often attracted to the Alliance and other smaller parties which don't get as many people into Parliament.

(c) Fewer women have the sort of professional jobs in law, business, higher education and so on which provide experience useful in public life.

(d) Politics emphasises competitiveness and even aggression. There have been studies of children at play which suggest that boys tend to enjoy competition while girls prefer to co-operate. In one experiment where boys and girls had to persuade their peers to eat some unpleasant-tasting biscuits, the boys used a mixture of bullying and lies, whereas the girls promised a share of the reward and personal friendship. This might well suggest that in politics, males will be more successful.

(e) Women lack ambition for a career in public life. They get their satisfactions elsewhere – running a home and looking after their children. After all, these activities are the ones which society approves of for women. Men who do these jobs are regarded as slightly strange; women who prefer the demands of public life are thought of as being ever so slightly 'unnatural'. Society brings subtle pressures to bear so that female political ambition can easily become blunted.

(f) Women still do the majority of the work in the home and take the major responsibility for child care. Until men are prepared to take an equal share in all aspects of domestic life, it will be hard for women to give the 100% commitment which a life in politics requires.

Discuss the truth of these arguments.

Do you think different laws might be passed if there were more women MPs?

What could be done to encourage more women to go into national politics?

3 | Who does what in the home?

	Great Britain								Percentages
	Married people						Never-married people		
	Actual allocation of tasks			Tasks should be allocated to			Tasks should be allocated to		
	Mainly man	Mainly woman	Shared equally	Mainly man	Mainly woman	Shared equally	Mainly man	Mainly woman	Shared equally
Household tasks *(percentage allocation)*									
Washing and ironing	1	88	9	-	77	21	-	68	30
Preparation of evening meal	5	77	16	1	61	35	1	49	49
Household cleaning	3	72	23	-	51	45	1	42	56
Household shopping	6	54	39	-	35	62	-	31	68
Evening dishes	18	37	41	12	21	64	13	15	71
Organisation of household money and bills	32	38	28	23	15	58	19	16	63
Repairs of household equipment	83	6	8	79	2	17	74	-	24
Child-rearing *(percentage allocation)*									
Looks after the children when they are sick	1	63	35	-	49	47	-	48	50
Teaches the children discipline	10	12	77	12	5	80	16	4	80

As part of the 1985 statistical survey, married people and those who had never been married were asked how various household and child-rearing tasks should be allocated between husband and wife.

Use the figures given in the table above to answer the following questions:

(a) In the actual allocation of tasks in the home, which household tasks are mainly done by women and which by men?
(b) Which is the task least favoured by men and which by women?
(c) Which task is most evenly shared?
(d) Compare how married people felt about how tasks should be allocated with what happened in practice. What grievances do the figures suggest?

(e) Look at the figures given for the opinions of never married people. Where do their views differ most from what actually happens?

General questions

(f) How do the figures given in columns 1 and 3 compare with your own experience?
(g) From your own experience, how much do you think the allocation of tasks will change in the next decade?
(h) The table doesn't give any information about tasks performed by the children in these households. From your experience, which tasks are done by children? Is there any difference between the household tasks done by boys and girls?

4 | **Little boys and little girls**

NATURAL HISTORY

WHAT are little boys made of, made of?
What are little boys made of?
    Frogs and snails
    And puppy-dogs' tails,
That's what little boys are made of.

What are little girls made of, made of?
What are little girls made of?
    Sugar and spice
    And all things nice,
That's what little girls are made of.

What are young men made of, made of?
What are young men made of?
    Sighs and leers
    And crocodile tears,
That's what young men are made of.

What are young women made of, made of?
What are young women made of?
    Ribbons and laces
    And sweet pretty faces,
That's what young women are made of.

(a) What roles are usually given to boys and girls in books, comics or on television? For example, who are the leaders in most activities? Who demonstrates gentleness? Who is tough?
(b) How do you think young children learn to act in masculine or feminine ways? How much influence do you think children's song and story books have? Do you think these books should be vetted by schools and libraries?

5

Men Talk

(Rap)

Women
Rabbit rabbit rabbit women
Tattle and titter
Women prattle
Women waffle and witter

Men Talk. Men Talk.

Women into Girl Talk
About Women's Trouble
Trivia 'n' Small Talk
They yap and they babble

Men Talk. Men Talk.

Women yatter
Women chatter
Women chew the fat, women spill the beans
Women aint been takin'
The oh-so Good Advice in them
Women's Magazines.

A Man Likes A Good Listener.

Oh Yeah
I like A Woman
Who likes me enough
Not to nitpick
Not to nag and
Not to interrupt 'cause I call that treason
A woman with the Good Grace
To be struck dumb
By me Sweet Reason. Yes –

A Man Likes a Good Listener

A Real
Man
Likes a Real Good Listener
Women yap yap yap
Verbal Diarrhoea is a Female Disease
Woman she spread rumours round she
Like Philadelphia Cream Cheese.

Oh
Bossy Women Gossip
Girlish Women Giggle
Women natter, women nag
Women niggle niggle niggle

Men Talk.

Men
Think First, Speak Later
Men Talk.

Liz Lochhead

In small groups work out your own 'rap' on some aspect of the relationships between men and women. ('Rap' – a rhythmic, colloquial, oral expression of feelings and ideas.)

6   Research project: popular images of boys and girls

(a) Find as many examples as you can from books, comics or magazines of boys and girls being given stereotyped roles. For example, you might look at early reading books, boys' and girls' comics, popular story books and so on.

(b) Find some examples from books, comics and magazines where boys and girls act outside the usual stereotypes. For example, a story where a boy looks after a group of young children on his own.

FASHION AND STYLE

1	**Suffering to be beautiful**

The clothes which fashionable ladies wore in Victorian times were designed to express the accepted view of 'true femininity'. For much of the period women wore long, full dresses, later known as crinolines. These were originally held out by layers and layers of petticoats, and the effect was to show off their tiny waists (above). Girls used to starve and corset themselves to achieve a 'hand-span' waist of 17 inches! In 1850, an American, Miss Amelia Bloomer, invented a new and much more comfortable type of dress. It was warmly recommended in Eliza Cook's journal, 1851: *Every surgeon knows well enough what destruction to female life and health have been caused by the use of stays and corsets, since the popular notion of being charming has been confined to a handbreadth of tightly compressed ribs and liver. What would the ladies say – to adopting the New American female dress? The upper garment is loose-fitting and reaches to the knees; underneath are loose trousers reaching to the ankles. The new dress is greatly approved by those who wear it . . .*
A few daring young ladies took this advice, but the fashion was soon laughed out of existence, because most men thought it was unfeminine. Women returned to the confinement of their crinolines which were now supported by even less comfortable steel hoops. By the late 1860s these skirts had become so wide that it was almost impossible for anyone to get through a door wearing them, and they were hitched up behind to form a new fashion, the bustle.

(a) What discomforts are you prepared to endure to look fashionable? For example, having your ears pierced, wearing uncomfortable shoes, dyeing your hair?

(b) How do you justify the time you take over your appearance?

(c) How do you think today's fashion reflects the ideas and feelings of society? For example, the wider use of casual clothes probably reflects the increasing emphasis on physical fitness and leisure.

2 Is fashion just a commercial racket?

Read the debate on fashion on pages 87–90. Which of the arguments do you find most convincing?

3 Freedom of dress

Does anyone have the right to tell you what to wear?

(a) Should employers dictate the kind of clothes worn by employees?

(b) What kind of rules do your parents impose on what you wear?

(c) What kind of rules does your school impose?

(d) What benefits are there in wearing a uniform? For example, there have been experiments where nurses were asked to wear ordinary clothes for work.

(e) 'The College welcomes the originality and novelty which students show in their dress, but it must be appropriate to their course of study and not cause offence or tension within the community.' Quote from College handbook.

Are there any limits on acceptable clothing – for example, should people be allowed to wear political insignia? What are the limits of decency in male and female dress on or off the beach?

4   What is an image?

> One of the new generation of design merchants is Paul Smith . . . He knew that in the new design world, the trend would be for total merchandising. So alongside suits and shirts and socks, Smith peddled watches, pens and cigarette lighters, torches, penknives and calculators. The fashionably dressed young-man-about-town soon learned his lesson: well-cut trousers are not enough, style victory could only be won through accessories. (*Sunday Times*, 23.2.86)

Think of three or four different kinds of images you have come across. What 'accessories' do people with these images possess? For example, the 'stars' in young people's magazines often given interviews where they talk about their lifestyle. What do they say about what they eat, drink, drive, wear or think which adds up to a particular image?

5   Research project: 50 years of fashions and styles

Obtain material for a report on the changes in fashion which have taken place over the last 50 years.

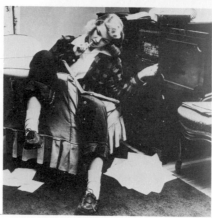

(a) Talk to people of different ages and ask them what clothes, hairstyles, make-up and objects were fashionable when they were abut 16. For example, between 1955 and 1960, winkle pickers, stiletto heels, beehives, gingham and hooped petticoats were all fashionable.

(b) Find out what the main 'looks' have been in the last 50 years. For example, the mini skirt and the 'austerity' look of the 1940s.

(c) Find out about the history of big stores like Marks and Spencer and Habitat. How do you think they have affected people's ideas of style and fashion in clothes, furniture and even food?

(d) Make a list of styles in clothes, hair, make-up and objects which are in fashion at the moment. How do you think things will change in the next few years?

SECTION 4

VIOLENCE

1 | Violence in toys and fairytales

In this article, Jack Straw considers the influence of certain toys on his son.

It was 3.20 pm on the Thursday before Christmas 1984 when I finally conceded that, in the battle for my son's soul, Mattel Inc had won.

Mattel is a toymaker, manufacturer of He-Man, Man-E-Faces, Ram Man, Skeletor, Tri-Klops, Trap Jaw, Mer-Man, Beast Man, Zodac and every other character in the Masters of the Universe. I hate the lot of them. Last year, these figures (priced around £3 each) had taken over half the ground floor of Hamley's in Regent Street and the entire imagination of my son and his friends. This year, He-Man and his friends have been relegated to the basement (the ground floor being filled with soft and cuddly toys, including a large elephant, price £1,125): but they still grip my son, and his friends. I still hate them.

No doubt I should see a psychiatrist about my obsessive dislike of Masters of the Universe. After all, when I was a child, I devoured war comics, graduating from *Beano* and *Dandy* to the *Eagle*. (*Hotspur*, beloved of the *Economist*, was quite beyond me – all words and no pictures.) I acted out fantasies, became a member of a playground gang and made forts in Epping Forest opposite my primary school. But, even allowing for my middle age, and the softening of my childhood recollections, there is something different about Masters of the Universe. The whole appalling series has but one characteristic – it glorifies gratuitous violence.

He-Man, and the rest of them, are plastic models, expensive and very well made (usually in Taiwan). They have been brilliantly marketed. Each comes with a comic in which the character just purchased features prominently. Their attraction to children aged five or so is reinforced by a television cartoon

shown regularly throughout the year.

Mattel Inc is proud of its creation. He-Man won a top toy award in 1983. It says, in answer to this prissy protective parent, that all its toys are produced in line with 'child guidance principles' (though it agrees that no psychological studies of the impact of the toys have been conducted).

The world of Masters of the Universe is divided into goodies and baddies. He-Man is a large muscular Aryan; his companion, Princess Rana, a white-skinned busty brunette. He-Man's arch opponent, Skeletor, is coloured blue, with a green-yellow face of a skeleton.

The story line in all the comics is simple. An associated goodie is put in mortal danger by Skeletor, Evil Lord of Destruction. Along comes He-Man who, by the power of Grayskull, becomes the most powerful man in the universe, and saves the day. A typical page contains the following dialogue:
'Kazam' 'You not taking ANYONE ANYWHERE'
'GROW-ROARRR'
'FIGHT! FIGHT!'
'BATTLE CAT. Get the girl, I'll fend off these CREATURES'
'SNARL GRRR'
'DESTROY, KILL'
'TASTE the power of GRAYSKULL',
and on it goes.

Mattel justifies this nonsense by saying that the design is based on a 'good versus evil' theme, and that the good guy always wins. In a literal sense, that is true, since the characters labelled 'good' always do win, despite the fact that they have hacked to death a large number of baddies who, being baddies, have no feelings, no ideas, no status, and who self-evidently deserve to lose.

But what a perverted idea of

morality if conveys. The message is simple: might is right: the strongest always win: and by chance, the strongest also happen to be the most beautiful, male and white. Good is only good because it is labelled good. This series is America at its most grotesque, most right-wing.

Of course, all children seek to identify with powerful, fantastic characters. It is one way they come to terms with the horrifying life-and-death power which the adult world exerts over them, with the all-pervading sense of dependence and fear which grown-ups can induce. This is one reason why fairy tales have been so timeless in their appeal; and why a writer like Roald Dahl so cleverly captures children's imaginations, with works like *Charlie and the Chocolate Factory*, and *The Enormous Crocodile*.

There are three characteristics of fairy tales or good modern children's stories, however, which distinguish them from the unceasing brutality of the Masters of the Universe. The first is humour, or at least some expression of human frailty; the second is that the weak or the unattractive or the poor may prosper in the end; that native wit and brainpower, combined with goodness, can outsmart the evil or brute force. The third is wonder.

'If you really read the fairy tales, you will observe that one idea runs from one end of them to the other – the idea that peace and happiness can only exist on some condition', wrote G. K. Chesterton. 'This idea, which is the core of ethics, is the core of the nursery tale.' There is nothing ethical about He-Man: just undiluted violence. When television violence is cleared off the screen, then maybe these appalling toys had better be cleared away too.

The author is Labour MP for Blackburn.

(a) Do you think children should be allowed to play with violent toys, to read stories which admire violent behaviour or to watch violent programmes on television? What effects do you think these have on the way they behave?

(b) Can you think of any children's stories which fulfil the three conditions Jack Straw outlines in his penultimate paragraph?

'The first is humour, or at least some expression of human frailty; the second is that the weak or unattractive or the poor may prosper in the end; that native wit and brainpower, combined with goodness, can outsmart the evil of brute force. The third is wonder.'

(c) See if you can work together to think of a story or a set of characters suitable for a comic book which would fulfil these three conditions *and* appeal to small children.

2 Self-defence

(a) Should all young people know how to defend themselves? What are the possible dangers of using self-defence techniques?

(b) Should self-defence techniques be taught at school as part of the regular PE programme? What objections might be raised?

(c) How far should you go when defending yourself?

(d) How useful are the martial arts in resisting attack?

(e) What precautions can you take against mugging and personal attack?

(f) How do you think girls and women can deal with sexual harassment, either physical or verbal?

3	**Arming the police**

Plastic and rubber bullets: current use

Up to November 1981 a total of about 43,000 plastic bullets were fired in Northern Ireland; 55,000 rubber bullets were fired during the period 1970 to 1975. Rubber bullets claimed the lives of three people and up to November 1981 plastic bullets killed 11 people (the twelfth victim was John Downes who was killed in August 1984). The age of these victims ranged from 10 to 45, but six of the 12 were children aged 15 and under.

The death rate from rubber bullets was one for every 18,000 rounds fired; for plastic bullets it is one for every 4000 rounds fired. Plastic bullets are more than four times as lethal as the weapons they replaced. The rate of serious injuries is also dramatically up.

A survey conducted by the staff at the Royal Victoria Hospital in Belfast between 1970 and 1972 showed 90 cases needing treatment as a result of 33,000 rubber bullets fired during this period. By comparison government figures reveal 110 cases needing hospital treatment between May and June 1981 during which time 17,000 plastic bullets were fired. Injuries from both weapons are similar in type: they include skull fractures, blinding, brain damage, fractures to the jaw and limbs, wounds requiring up to 40 stitches and damage to the body's internal organs.

Many of the victims of plastic bullets were clearly innocent of any criminal activity. Inquests have found that six of the 12 killed were not involved in any disturbances which may have been going on at the time; there are others against whom allegations of stone-throwing have been made, but the penalty for this is not death.

Regulations which govern the use of plastic bullets in Northern Ireland state that they should be aimed at the lower part of the body and not used at ranges less than 20 metres 'except where the safety of soldiers or others is threatened'. Even if these regulations were observed plastic bullets can still kill and maim, but these regulations are routinely breached. For example, of the 12 people killed by plastic bullets all died from head or chest injuries. There is no way that regulations can safeguard the use of plastic bullets.

(a) Sum up the arguments against the use of plastic bullets which are made in this extract.

What arguments can you think of in favour of the police using plastic bullets?

(b) Think of as many arguments as you can both for and against arming the police. What incidents have happened in the last two or three years which might support either side of the argument? For example, there was a case where a policeman killed a 5-year-old boy when his gun went off accidently during a raid. On another occasion, an unarmed policeman was shot during a riot.

4 **Vandals and hooligans**

'The only way to teach vandals and hooligans to behave is by taking the strap to them. What they need is a good beating.' Do you think there is any truth in this statement?

5 **Research project: crime trends in your area**

Obtain information for a report on crime in your area.

Visit a local magistrates court. Note the type of case most frequently brought. Note the kind of sentences given. Talk to one or more magistrates to get their opinions.

Look through copies of your local paper for the last few months and note the criminal cases that got into the news.

Talk to your local police – what do they think could be done to improve crime prevention, particularly among young people?

1   **Children and competitive sport**

Too much too young?

Are our children playing sport too hard?

IF YOU were reared on that fine British tradition of forging an excuse note for the gym teacher or praying for snow on sports day, you'll be shocked by the news that some of our youngsters are being burned out by too much competitive sport.

We have all heard that Tracy Austin played too much too early on the international tennis circuit and is now retired. But intensive and dangerous stress-inducing sports training is surely only a phenomenon of the United States or the communist countries.

In Thursday's **Children in Sport**, a documentary and phone-in, researcher and presenter Wendy Lloyd promises to reach those parts we non-sporting types are best at exercising – the eyebrows. Britain's schoolchildren and teenagers are in danger from ignorant coaching, over-ambitious parents and an increasing obsession, in some quarters, on winning at all costs.

'There are plenty of British youngsters whose physical development has been impeded and damaged by participation in sport too early,' says Wendy. 'There are orthopaedic injuries to bones that are still growing, irreparable damage to cartilages in the back and chronic injuries. through over-use . . . the list is frightening.'

Another common finding has been that many of the coaches are not trained properly. 'So many are just gifted amateurs. Lots are enthusiastic parents or friendly ex-athletes who haven't been trained with the child's welfare in mind.'

Then there's the vexed question of competitiveness itself. Is it a good thing to introduce your child to the bitter flavour of defeat so early on, to encourage an obsession to win? 'I'm a competitive person myself,' admits Wendy. 'I love to win and hate to lose. But I got a shock last summer when I played in my local Lawn Tennis

Association rating tournament. I was doing fine until I got to my section's semi-finals when I was knocked out by a 12-year-old. She was very tense and showing the sort of tensions at 12 which I would be unhappy to see had it been my own daughter.'

Wendy's victor was only one year younger than British swimmer Zara Long, who made her name as our youngest competitor in the last Olympics. 'She came home just about burnt out. She'd made the team, she'd taken part but she didn't come home with a medal. She'd achieved so much, so young, yet she'd had so much stress. Up at 5.30 every morning to drive with her parents to Croydon baths. Eight thousand metres before breakfast. The same performance after school. Can you imagine it?'

But Zara didn't go up in smoke. She's now at a special sports-orientated boarding school. Her hours don't have to cover tedious travelling between pool and base, her coach is able to fit in a more sympathetic routine and she's able to get down seriously to O-levels as well as swimming.

If Zara's happier, can it compare with her parents' extra two hours in bed each morning? 'You get two types of parents, it seems,' says Wendy. 'The type who never fulfilled their own ambition when young and who are determined to push and push. Then there are those who, like the Longs, will make every sacrifice for a child who is very talented and competitive.'

In her own household of three young daughters, Wendy Lloyd might be relieved to admit she only has one who's both sporty and competitive. 'She's just started short tennis for fun and enjoys it. But I dare say she might be swept up in tennis or something else if she's very, very good. That's when we'd have to look carefully at it.' ●

(a) Should there be a minimum age at which children can compete in major competitions?

(b) Do you think there should be less emphasis on *competitive* sport in schools? Are there any sports which place less emphasis on competition and more on individual achievement?

(c) Why do you think sport is compulsory at school?

(d) Should there be more sports orientated schools (like the one mentioned in the article) to cater for gifted young players?

2　**Anything to win**

These are some of the ways in which athletes have tried to boost their performance:

– Blood transfusions for cyclists just before a race.

– Anabolic steroids for shot putters.

– Training at high altitudes for runners.

(a) What sort of help should athletes be permitted in training? For example, is training at altitude acceptable? How much help should a coach be allowed to give from the sidelines?

(b) Should it be left to the athletes themselves to decide if they are going to affect their own health and future well-being?

(c) Do you think the desire to win, whether for yourself or for your country, can justify artificially aiding your performance?

(d) Are sophisticated training methods unfair on poorer nations?

3 **Sport for life**

(a) Most people give up sport when they leave school. Can you think of ways of encouraging people to continue with a sport or sports?

(b) What sports facilities are there in your area for people of all ages to play sport?

4 **What is a sport?**

(a) Are these sports?
  – Synchronised swimming
  – Ice dancing
  – Rambling
  – Gymnastic floor exercises
  – Beauty contests
  – Dog fighting
  – Monopoly
  – Chess

(b) Can you invent some new sports?

5 **Sport and politics**

(a) 'There's no point in trying to separate international sport from politics.' Think of as many examples as you can of different sports being affected by political action or points of view. For example, the boycott of sporting links with South Africa.

(b) Should sport and politics be kept separate? Why? Or why not?

(c) Do you think international sports competitions would be improved if medal league tables, national anthems, processions under national flags and so on were abolished?

(d) How could conflict between fans of rival clubs or teams be reduced?

6 | **Research project: sport now and in the future**

Obtain information for a report on the sports of the future. Conduct a survey of as many different kinds of people as possible – for example, you should ask people of all ages, from 9 to 90, for their opinions. Find out the opinion of specialists on all the questions – for example, you could ask the PE staff at your school and the person responsible for sport and recreation in your local council.

(a) Find out if men and women have different attitudes towards sport. Do they want different things?
(b) What different needs do spectators and participants have?
(c) What new sports are growing in popularity?
(d) Which sports are declining?
(e) What reasons can you find out for these changes?
(f) Find out about levels of attendance at local swimming pools and sports centres. Have more people been going swimming than in previous years? Are people doing different kinds of sports – for example, have more classes started in martial arts in the last 5 years? Has there been a greater demand for squash courts?
(g) Find out how sports coverage on TV has changed in the last 5, 10 and 20 years. What influence has this had on the sports people play? Do more or fewer people become live spectators of sports now shown on TV – or do they just stay at home to watch them on the box?
(h) Make recommendations for new sports facilities in your area. Suggest ways in which school sports facilities could be used by the rest of the community.
(i) How do you think sport is going to develop over the next 5 or 10 years?

1

The price of education

Read the article on the opposite page and then answer the questions below.

(a) Imagine a scene in Ratiram's home. What do you think would be said and done? What feelings would each of the family have about what was happening?

(b) 'What, Ratiram asked, was the good of a town education? The boy would return with strange ideas – "if he returns at all" – and would regard work in the fields as beneath him.'

   In what ways do you think education causes rifts within families and communities?

(c) Is education a right?

(d) Victor Zorza, who wrote this piece, has chosen to go to live in a Himalayan village and writes regularly about his life there for a British newspaper. What difficulties do you think he encounters?

The Times 10/3/86

Village Voice

Father's ambition for son thwarted by family illness

Victor Zorza this week describes from his Himalayan village the plight of a father who wants his intelligent son to have a good education but is thwarted by the drain on his meagre resources of illness in the family.

My neighbour's son was always hanging around my hut with other village children, but he was different. While they observed my strange ways silently, Prakash never stopped asking questions. Why did I eat with a fork when everybody used their fingers? Why did I boil my water? He was far more intelligent than the other boys and could go far, I told his father – but only if he sent him away to be educated.

Should he send his son to a government school, the farmer-priest asked, or to a religious *ashram* where he would be taught Sanskrit? With the learning acquired at the *ashram*, he said, Prakash would be much sought after for priestly duties and would be generously rewarded. Ratiram, his father, would be well looked after in his old age.

What, Ratiram asked, was the good of a town education? The boy would return with strange ideas – "if he returns at all" – and would regard work in the fields as beneath him. Ratiram had obviously made up his mind and had come to ask my advice only out of politeness. He did not want me to feel that he had rejected a neighbour's counsel, without giving it full consideration. But there was still a year or two to go before Prakash would be ready to leave the village. His father might yet change his mind.

I hoped that if Prakash did go to school, and perhaps even to college, he might acquire the education and the self-assurance which would enable him to help the community, speak to officials on its behalf, and protect it from outsiders who came to exploit it. He was not yet in his teens but wise beyond his years. His intelligence and strength of character, I thought, should enable him to absorb the best that education had to offer. I might be wrong, though, and must not interfere.

But leave the village he would, for the *ashram* if not for the school, and Ratiram had long been saving the money that would be needed. It was not easy. He was poorer than most of the village Brahmins, and the family survived on a diet of rice and lentils barely sufficient to keep body and soul together. The last harvest has been poor and the new crop had not yet ripened.

They managed without essentials like kerosene for the lamp and without matches, using flint and tinder to light the kitchen fire. Fuel was free, for Ratiram gathered firewood on the hills, though it might often take a whole day to procure a week's supply. This was woman's work, but their year-old baby had fallen ill and someone had to stay with it all the time. The evil spirit which had entered the child refused to be exorcised by magic. Ratiram first tried a quack and then an Ayurvedic physician who prescribed herbal potions, but all to no avail. Finally he braved the unfamiliar hazards of a long journey to a doctor in town.

The baby was half the size it should have been and the doctor had concluded that the constant vomiting had deprived it of the nutrition it needed. The drugs he prescribed helped, but the improvement was short-lived. Ratiram's repeated journeys to town, the bus fares, the medicines, took time and money he could ill afford. He did what work he could in the fields, but I often saw him pacing up and down the lane, rocking the crying baby in his arms, while his wife was busy with the cooking and other chores.

Savings spent to buy two tins of powdered milk

Less work in the fields would mean a smaller crop and even less food for the family and nutrition for the baby. It was not long before the child's illness had consumed almost all they had saved for Prakash's education.

In a shop window in town, when Ratiram had taken the child to the doctor, he had seen tins of powdered milk adorned with a happy, smiling baby's face – a fatter baby, he told me, than he ever laid his eyes upon. This, he said, was the nutrition his child lacked, and he used the last of his savings to buy a couple of tins.

But the baby still cannot keep its food down. Several other village infants, similarly afflicted, have not survived. This is the youngest of his four children. Prakash is the eldest. He had two more, but they died.

Ratiram and his wife are in their early thirties and will no doubt have more children. But Ratiram no longer talks of his plans for Prakash. "We'll never be able to save enough," he says, "and if we do, it'll go like this lot has. There's always some misfortune or other."

The boy will probably go neither to school in town nor to the *ashram*. He still visits my hut, but sits listlessly in the corner.

He asks no more questions.

© **Victor Zorza 1986**

Victor Zorza thanks readers who have sent money for needy villagers and requests that any future donations should be sent not to him but to the Village Voice Fund, Oxfam, 274 Banbury Road, Oxford.

2

Helping the third world

Jane Tewson is director of the innovative fund-raising company, Charity Projects. She doesn't believe in conscience-salving pennies for the poor. She believes in action . . .

Tewson went to the Sudan to see the famine situation at first hand. There was only one main road and she made her way around by hitching lifts in Save the Children Fund trucks. When she arrived at Wad Kawali on the Ethiopian border she was greeted with open arms because they thought she was a nurse. They didn't have any and there had been an influx of 4000 new refugees.

On her first day there she saw a child suffering from rabies. She stayed and was put to work sorting out the worst affected children, garbing them in Save the Children T-shirts and sending them to a feeding centre. 'Then I got viral penumonia', she said, immediately dismissing five weeks of solid hard work, 'followed by treatment resistant malaria' . . .

Six years ago Jane Tewson, now 27, came to London from Buckinghamshire. She had written to Mencap with an idea for an arts fair and they had replied immediately, inviting her to join as a secretary the next day. Very soon she became projects coordinator. She worked on the premise that the more accessible an event is, the more the public is likely to learn from it and the more money you are likely to raise.

Her projects were fun and, unlike many charity benefits, didn't lose money, largely because the running costs were sponsored . . .

Two years ago she started Charity Projects with the help of Linda Batt-Rawden. It is a limited company with charitable status, but holds out no begging bowls. Rather, it uses the services of artists, performers and businessmen, and organises them to create products and events which it sells to the public for a profit. Every penny raised goes to specially defined uses, within the realm of carefully chosen charities . . .

Tewson has changed the style of charity, with any luck for ever. 'I don't see charities as dull and boring. I see sponsorship as being of great marketing value' . . .

In the Sudan, 'I had a child die in my arms and I could see in the mother's face the acceptance. It was the moment I had dreaded and had nightmares about, before going. Then suddenly it happened and I just went on to the next child. A little later I saw a healthy man drinking a child's milk and I just walked over and whacked him. I'm not a violent person. It was just my pent-up feelings about the death'

(a) If you decided you wanted to help people suffering from famine, what would you do?

(b) How would you describe Jane Tewson's ideas about fund-raising for charity? Do you agree with her?

(c) 'I had a child die in my arms and I could see on the mother's face the acceptance. It was the moment I had dreaded and had nightmares about, before going. Then suddenly it happened and I just went on to the next child. A little later I saw a healthy man drinking a child's milk and I just walked over and whacked him.'

We all have our own code of right behaviour. How do you think this might have to change in extreme circumstances? For example, how might you justify the man drinking the child's milk or Jane Tewson hitting him for doing so?

3 Famine and plenty

'While one part of the world is struggling for enough to eat, the other part is obsessed with slimming.'

What can be done about it?

4 Population control

In China, no family is allowed to have more than one child. In India, men have been encouraged to have vasectomies to limit their family size.

Are we justified in telling other people to limit the size of their families?

5 Research project: another country

Work in groups or as individuals. Choose a country in the developing world. Find out as much as you can about its people and their culture and customs. Then make notes for a talk to the rest of the class describing aspects of life in your chosen country. If you can, use maps, pictures and so on to illustrate your talk. You could if you want, choose to tell an imaginary story of one particular family and what happens to them on a typical day, using the information you've found. Or, if you're working in a group, you could role play some events from their everyday life.

For information, write to or phone the public relations departments of embassies, tourists offices, big charities or the Commonwealth Institute in London. Ask in your library for appropriate reference books.

LOST AT SEA

These are the answers according to the experts of the US Marines. They are not necessarily any more 'right' than your own answers, though you may be interested in some of their reasons.

1 SHAVING MIRROR: signalling air–sea rescue.
2 2-GALLON CAN OF OIL/PETROL MIXTURE: signalling by making a fire outside raft.
3 5-GALLON CAN OF WATER: more important than food.
4 ARMY 'C' RATIONS: basic food intake.
5 20 FEET OF OPAQUE PLASTIC: shelter/collect rain water.
6 2 BOXES OF CHOCOLATE BARS: reserve food supply.
7 FISHING KIT: lower than chocolate on the 'bird-in-hand' principle.
8 15-FOOT NYLON ROPE: lash equipment together and life line.
9 SEAT CUSHION: act as lifebuoy if man overboard.
10 SHARK REPELLENT: obvious!
11 QUART OF 160 PROOF RUM: antiseptic (not to drink – heat loss/dehydration).
12 TRANSISTOR RADIO: not much use – no transmitter.
13 MAPS OF PACIFIC OCEAN: useless without additional navigation equipment.
14 MOSQUITO NETTING: no mosquitoes in mid-Pacific!
15 SEXTANT: no use without tables/chronometer.

DEBATING RULES

1 How to set the room out.

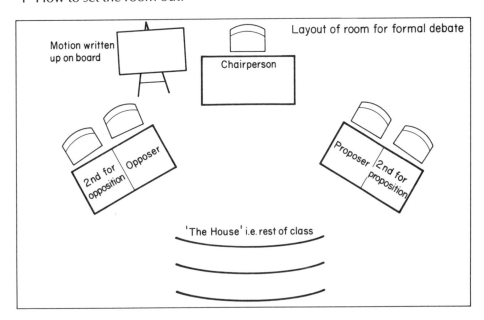

Layout of room for formal debate

Motion written up on board

Chairperson

2nd for opposition | Opposer

Proposer | 2nd for proposition

'The House' i.e. rest of class

2 Order of events:

(a) The Chair calls the House to order and announces the motion (i.e. subject) to be discussed. The motion traditionally starts with the words 'This House . . .' (e.g. 'This House believes that . . .' or 'This House disapproves of . . .') The Chair introduces all four speakers and then 'calls upon' the Proposer to speak first.

(b) The Proposer stands up and speaks in support of the motion. S/he should start by explaining how the Proposition is going to deal with the topic – what their main arguments will be. The Proposer ends by asking the House to vote for the motion.

(c) The Chair thanks the Proposer and calls upon the Opposer to speak.

(d) The Opposer stands up and speaks against the motion. S/he should explain how the Opposition is going to deal with the topic. The Opposer should also refute – i.e. contradict – the arguments of the Proposer using skilful arguments of his/her own.

(e) The Chair thanks the Opposer and calls upon the Seconder to the Proposition to speak.

(f) The Seconder to the Proposition stands up and continues the arguments of the Proposer and refutes the arguments of the Opposer. S/he summarises the case for the motion and asks for the support of the House.

(g) The Chair thanks the Seconder to the Proposition and calls upon the Seconder to the Opposition to speak.

(h) The Seconder to the Opposition stands up and continues the arguments of the Opposer. S/he also attacks the Proposition's theories and ends by summarising the case against the motion.

(i) The Chair thanks the Seconder to the Opposition and 'opens the discussion to the floor of the House.' Anyone may now speak when invited to do so by the Chair. The Chair should make sure that ideas are put forward on both sides of the argument.

(j) The Chair asks the Opposer to sum up for the Opposition.

(k) The Opposer sums up, answering points raised by the speakers from the floor and appeals, giving reasons, to the House to vote against the motion.

(l) The Chair asks the Proposer to sum up for the Proposition.

(m) The Proposer sums up as in (k) above and appeals to the House to support the motion.

(n) The Chair asks two people to act as tellers to help count the votes accurately. The Chair then repeats the motion and counts the votes. These can be FOR, AGAINST or ABSTENTIONS (people who can't decide how to vote or who wish to abstain from expressing a view).

(o) The Chair announces the result of the debate.

3 Suggested timing:

Main speakers (Proposer and Opposer) .... 4 minutes each
Seconders .... 2/3 minutes each
Contributions from the floor (aim at everyone making a comment) .... 15/20 minutes
Summing up (main speakers only) .... 2 minutes each

This would take about 40–45 minutes altogether including introductions.